STANDING AT THE EDGE OF THE WATER

To Victoria

John V. Morgan

JOHN V. MORGAN

ISBN: 978-1-939779-29-8 (Print Version)
ISBN: 978-1-939779-30-4 (Ebook)

Published by

LIFEBRIDGE
B O O K S
P.O. BOX 49428
CHARLOTTE, NC 28277

DEDICATION

To the memory of my Dad and Mom.

*Throughout your lives I watched as time after
time you came to the water's edge and with courage
and confidence kept moving forward. You were faithfully
committed to the cause of Christ, and He was ever faithful
to make a way. Your example continues as an encouragement, inspiration, and challenge to all who knew you. Your
children and children's children—both natural and
spiritual—rise up and call you blessed.*

To my beloved Betsy.

*My staunchest supporter, greatest fan,
loudest cheerleader, and closest confidante.
You continue to believe in me even in those times when
I don't believe in myself. You challenge me to dream and
to pursue those dreams, knowing you'll be there with me
whether they succeed or fail. You're the best! I don't
have words to adequately express how thankful I am
that God has put us together. I love you—more.*

3

ACKNOWLEDGMENTS

In the writing and publishing of this book I've been blessed with an incredible network of support and encouragement.

Many thanks to the team at Life Bridge Books who believed in this project and with skill far beyond my ability have taken my rough material and carefully crafted it into something presentable to the reading public. Any errors are solely mine—and more than likely due to a stubborn unwillingness to follow their suggestions.

Thank you, Troy Miller, for the prayer. Gone way too soon—but never forgotten!

I owe such a debt of gratitude to some very special men and women who have inspired, encouraged, and challenged me in my journey. Over the years these people have prayed for me, counseled me, and each in their own unique manner has gone out of their way to affirm the call of God on my life. Some have already joined that great cloud of witnesses, urging us on in our race. Others remain; by their continued faithfulness they serve as role models and mentors for those who follow behind. Charles W. Conn, Carl Richardson, John Nichols, James Byrd, Randy and Annette Watson, Walter and Bobbie Lauster, and Jeanette Chesser are spiritual giants I am privileged to be able to call friends and to whom I give honor and thanks.

Special appreciation to the congregations of Praise Temple (now Parkway Life) in Naples, FL and Regency Church in Jacksonville, FL. You were the first ones to hear this material in sermon form and your enthusiastic response and expressed appreciation for those messages planted the seed that led to the publishing of this book. Your support, prayers, and responsiveness to the ministry are not something I ever take lightly. I thank my God upon every remembrance of you.

Finally, and most importantly, all praise to God—Father, Son, and Holy Spirit. To Him be all glory!

My prayer for all who read this work is that you will have ears to hear not so much what I am saying, but that you will hear the voice of the Spirit speaking through these pages.

ENDORSEMENTS

Pastor Morgan invites the reader to travel with him to some of the most memorable stories of the Old Testament. The common theme emphasized by the author is how these familiar narratives are connected by a defining historical event when God's servants stood *at the edge of the water.*

However, John does much more than narrate stories connected together by a common theme—even though he does indeed tell these stories with remarkable skill. With a true pastor's heart, he leads the readers into the inspiring and challenging decisions that believers face in life today *at the edge of the water.*

Throughout this remarkable journey, the author candidly relates personal stories which immediately unite the hearts of readers with the heart of the writer. But the excellent exegesis and application of biblical passages give an outstanding authenticity to this book that leads the sincere reader into the glorious presence of God.

I am pleased to recommend this splendid volume to all believers who yearn to draw closer to the Lord as they come to those memorable moments in their own lives when they also *stand at the edge of the water.*

– Dr. Mark L. Williams, General Overseer
Church of God, Cleveland, Tennessee

Great preaching is more than the mere performance of an hour. Much more. It is the revelation of a life.

There is no doubt in my own heart that the creative messages in this exciting new book by Master Pastor John V. Morgan will be transformational in what often become the really big moments in our lives.

John Morgan is one of my all-time favorite ministers of God. He is always contemporary but never trendy. His words resonate with the weight of eternity.

– Carl Richardson,
International Evangelist, Tampa, Florida

CONTENTS

FOREWORD

Defining moments. That's what comes to mind as I consider the theme and content of John V. Morgan's new book, *Standing At the Edge of the Water.*

Reading this will help you understand that how we respond to those defining moments determines the outcome of each of our lives. Sadly for some people, what could have been defining moments became "declining" moments. Coming to the edge of the water, intimidation confronted them and caution became a crippling paralysis.

Rather than passing through the water, the road of least resistance is chosen by many men and women. While the easy road may leave one safe, it also and often leads to being unfulfilled. Faith in God and confidence in His Word always makes the difference.

By carefully studying the experiences of Jacob, Joshua, Elijah, David, and others, John Morgan articulately describes many key principles of "forward living." This is life the way it was meant to be; fruitful, exhilarating, confident, trusting, and complete. In this book, John will take you to the edge of the water where reality is faced with trust, opportunity is faced with optimism, and adversity is faced with action.

The water is scary but exciting. It's deep but it's passable. Those ripples have rocks beneath them but they can be stepped on as you're crossing over. The chill is breathtaking but so is the view on the other side.

Don't run from it. Run into it. Whatever you do, don't be found tomorrow still standing there. It's time to move beyond the edge of the water and wade into the flow of God's abundant favor reserved for your life today. Don't miss your moment!

– Tim Hill
Director of World Missions, Church of God, Cleveland, TN

INTRODUCTION

The room was filled with pastors. Those with years of experience; novices in their first assignment; some serving large urban congregations, others in small rural communities with just a handful of parishioners. We had come together for the purpose of discussing challenges of ministry, to gain insight from one another, to "sharpen" our skills, and mostly to encourage each other in what can sometimes seem like a lonely journey.

At the beginning of the afternoon session a minister who has been a good friend for many years was asked to invoke God's blessings on our time together. He came to the front of the room and began to pray something like this, "Father, we've gathered here this afternoon, and some of us are at a place where we don't know whether we are facing the Red Sea or the Jordan..."

The Red Sea or the Jordan... I've been there. We've all been there at one time or another.

The Red Sea—surrounded by seemingly impossible odds. Can't move forward, can't go back. Can't turn to the right or to the left. Desperation on every side. Certain that the only available option is destruction. Wilderness to the side. Enemy behind, closing fast. Uncrossable obstacle in front. What seemed like following the voice of the Lord isn't panning out to be the glorious victory previously imagined. Yes, I've been there.

The Jordan—a future bright with hope and promise. Everything God has provided lies ahead. The wilderness wanderings behind. A new day, filled with possibilities, has dawned. Canaan is in sight, but it's just beyond our grasp because there remains one more river to cross. And we've never been this way before. Facing uncertainty. I've been there as well.

I confess I don't remember anything else about his prayer that day. But as I've spent time looking at the stories recorded in the pages of God's Word, I have been surprised at how often people in the Bible find themselves standing at the edge of a body of water—and that event becomes a defining moment in their lives.

The water's edge seems to be a pivotal place where, on one side things are one way, but then when you cross over to the other side, the world is completely different. The water's edge often becomes a point of challenge and a place of change in the lives of some of God's choice servants. At the water's edge there are significant lessons to learn—lessons that will encourage, inspire and challenge you on your journey.

Whether you are a new believer or a seasoned saint, I invite you to travel with me through the pages of this book to the edge of the water. God has divine lessons He wants to teach you and many powerful things He desires to do in your life.

The water's edge could very well be the place of breakthrough you've been needing. One thing is certain: once you've been to the edge of the water, life will never be the same again.

– John V. Morgan

CHAPTER 1

THE WATER OF DELIVERANCE

After a long, full day of hunting, Dad and my younger brother, Bruce, were heading home along a deserted stretch of remote highway. The dark clouds of a recent rainstorm had not yet dissipated, blocking out any light from moon and stars. No other traffic was present and the two weary hunters were looking forward to the end of their journey in the soft, warm comfort of their own beds.

As they approached the dead-end intersection where they were to turn right, Dad removed his foot from the accelerator and carefully applied the brakes. Unexpectedly, the brakes grabbed and the car began to spin out of control on the rain-slicked asphalt. On either side of the roadway were deep ditches, filled with water. In front was the end of the highway and beyond was a forest of trees. There was no stopping the car and no way to regain control.

Telling the story takes much longer than the actual event. It all happened so fast the only thing Dad could do was cry out, "Jesus help!"

Suddenly, it was as if a giant hand reached down, took hold of the car, lifted it up, and set it back down on the road, going in the direction they were planning to turn—completely under control. Dad and Bruce looked wide-eyed at each other and continued on their journey home, rejoicing in the Lord who had made a way where there didn't seem to be one. With nowhere to go, God had heard their cry for help and brought a miraculous deliverance.

DESPERATE FOR DELIVERANCE

Deliverance is such a powerful word. It's a robust word, bursting with possibilities. Deliverance enables us to escape the dark shackles of what lies behind and embrace the bright hope and promise of what lies ahead.

Deliverance doesn't come just because we have an intense desire for it. We can't wish for it and have it magically appear. When we are in bondage we can't free ourselves by any amount of personal struggle. Deliverance is only possible when the power that holds us captive is overcome by a power that is greater.

Whether we recognize it or not, each of us is in need of deliverance in two distinct areas. First, there is the need to be set free from the bondage of sin. Once that is accomplished, there is then the need for freedom from the power of both the temptation to return to our former paths and the spiritual enemy that would seek to place us back in sin's slavery once we have been liberated.

This isn't a modern phenomenon, but is a condition as old as humanity. In the ancient history of the people of God we find a story that vividly illustrates both the need and the provision of deliverance made for us by the Almighty.

After 400 years of slavery in Egypt, the desperate cries of the people of God reached a deafening crescendo. In the dramatic encounter with Moses at the burning bush God said, *"...I have surely seen the affliction of My people who are in Egypt, and have given heed to their cry because of their taskmasters, for I am aware of their sufferings. So I have come down to deliver them from the power of the Egyptians, and to bring them up from that land to a good and spacious land, to a land flowing with milk and honey..."* (Exodus 3:7-8).

In the story of Israel's rescue (Exodus 14:13-31), we're going to see a picture illustration of the deliverance that is offered to us today.

A RELEVANT STORY

The account of Israel's deliverance from Egypt is so familiar that I'm reluctant to spend much time rehearsing the details. In addition to reading it and hearing it taught and preached, you've probably also seen the Hollywood version with all the special effects, or the animated feature with incredible computer graphics. The characters are almost like family: Moses, Aaron, Miriam, and the children of Israel; Pharaoh, and the Egyptian army.

The problem with this kind of familiarity is that we often miss hearing the voice of the Spirit speaking to us because we feel like we already know what is about to happen next. What we sometimes forget is that this is more than a defining event in the life of the nation of Israel. It's more than an ancient history involving two Middle Eastern countries; in reality this is a contemporary tale—one that has practical application for where we live.

This account isn't preserved just so we can read it and be entertained. It isn't written so we can develop a script from it to be projected on the big screen. Instead, it is recorded to give us an example and has been faithfully handed down through the generations in order to teach us something of great importance (see 1 Corinthians 10:11).

The story begins with a famine in the land of Canaan and the children of Israel being preserved through divine intervention of God as He used what seemed at the time to be the horrible circumstances of Joseph to save His people from destruction. The saga continues with the passing of Joseph and his brothers and the eventual death of Pharaoh, until there arose in the land another Pharaoh who didn't remember Joseph and his dedicated service.

This Egyptian ruler began to oppress the people of God and made them slaves. Finally, after many long years of suffering and servitude, God sent Moses to be their deliverer.

You most likely will recall the scene of Moses and his confrontation with Pharaoh. See him striding into the palace and his voice commanding, "God...Jehovah...I Am...says, 'Let My people go.'"

Plagues came upon the land—one after another with increasing ferocity—all in an attempt to persuade Pharaoh to release the Israelites. After each plague, Pharaoh once again hardened his heart, refusing to release the people of God until the last, most horrific plague was visited on Egypt. All the first-born in the land were slain—both animal and human. But God made a special provision for His chosen people.

On the night in which the death angel was to pass through the land, all the Israelites took a first-born, spotless, unblemished lamb and sacrificed it. The blood of this animal was caught in a basin and then painted on the doorways of the houses in which they lived. The animal was roasted and eaten along with bitter herbs and unleavened bread.

Everything about this ritual was to remind the Israelites of the severity of their slavery, and cause them to realize the means by which their deliverance was accomplished. At the appointed time, the death angel came through the land of Egypt, killing all the first-born children. But when he saw a house painted with the blood of the sacrificial lamb, the angel passed over that home and the first-born was spared.

At the conclusion of this final plague, Pharaoh couldn't push the Israelites out of Egypt fast enough. So, in haste, the children of Israel left. They were saved from the death angel and released from the oppression and bondage of slavery—on their way to the land of promise which God had prepared for them.

They hadn't traveled very far down the road, however, before Pharaoh once more had a change of heart. He summoned all his army—and you can imagine how angry they were, because there wasn't one household of the Egyptians that was left untouched by the death angel. Once the forces were assembled and the chariots were mounted, they gave chase after the children of Israel, intent upon bringing them back to the bondage of Egypt.

THE TWO KINGDOMS

When the Bible talks about Egypt, it's referring to more than an ancient country and an early civilization. But in God's Word, Egypt is also used as a metaphor or a symbol of something spiritual. When Scripture speaks of Egypt, it uses that nation as a representation of sin and the bondage in which people are held by iniquity.

The message of the Bible is that each and every person on this planet is under the curse of sin and in need of deliverance from its slavery. That's the meaning of Romans 3:23: *"...for all* (no exclusionary clauses) *have sinned and fall short of the glory of God."* It is also the message of 1 John 1:8: *"If we say that we have no sin, we are deceiving ourselves and the truth is not in us."*

Every man, woman, and child is in need of a Savior—in need of someone capable of breaking the bondage of the cords of sin that are wrapped tightly around us.

- Sin blinds – it keeps us from seeing our need for help.
- Sin binds – it keeps us tied to that which will ultimately destroy not just our body, but also our soul.

Today, every person is a citizen of one of two kingdoms. You may think you are your own man; you may think you're your own woman—it just isn't so. You are in one of two camps, serving one of two masters. Either you are in God's glorious kingdom—that kingdom of light, serving Christ, or you're trapped in the kingdom of darkness, serving sin and Satan.

Only two choices; only two places. If you're not totally committed to being a Christ-follower—loving God with all your heart, mind, soul, and strength—then you're not part of His kingdom.

You may be what everybody calls a "good" person, a law-abiding citizen, an individual who is generous, kind, and loving. But if you have not put your trust in Jesus as the only hope of salvation, walking in that place where you've repented of your sin and surrendered your life to Christ, you are not living in God's kingdom. Instead, you're residing in the realm of darkness. Sin is in control—and is a harsh task-master. The path of sin will always lead to ruin and destruction.

But there is good news today. Just as God provided a means for Israel to be loosed from the bondage of her slavery in Egypt, He has provided a way for us to be freed from the bondage of sin—through the death of His only begotten Son on the cross of Calvary.

Jesus stated it clearly: *"I am the way, and the truth, and the life; no one comes to the Father but through Me"* (John 14:6).

THE REALITY

This is exactly the same idea we find in the story of the Exodus of the children of Israel. In that account we have the foreshadowing...the symbol. But now we have the reality.

- In the Exodus we have a sacrificial lamb. But now we have the perfect Lamb—the sinless, spotless, Lamb of God—Jesus Christ.
- In the Exodus, the lamb was slain and its blood was painted on the doorway of the house. But now, Jesus Christ has been slain. His blood was spilled on a rugged cross, and today, through faith in His name, that blood has been applied to the doorway of our hearts.
- In the Exodus, the children of Israel were released from Egypt. But now, we who have believed in Jesus Christ are released from the captivity of sin.
- In the Exodus, the death angel passed over the people of God. And now, when we come by faith in Jesus Christ, we have the assurance that we have been changed from death unto life. Old things are passed away; all things are become new. We are born again; we have an eternal inheritance with the saints —a glorious heritage that will never fade away!

The good news is that Jesus saves, but the bad news is that the devil isn't happy about it. He's going to do every-thing he can to bring us back into his kingdom, under his dominion.

Follow the Cloud!

As you continue reading, you discover that God didn't lead the Israelites by a direct route to the Promised Land of Canaan. Instead, once they crossed the border of Egypt, they took a hard right turn. There was a cloud by day and fire by night—God's holy presence with them manifested in the cloud and the fire. Israel didn't have to worry about the path or the direction they were taking. They had only one job—to follow the cloud.

It's been my observation that when God leads His people into the place of blessing and promise, He often doesn't take us there immediately. It can be a very circuitous route. Sometimes, in following the cloud of His presence, we find ourselves in the wilderness. But the issue is never whether or not we have reached our final destination. Rather, it is where we are in relationship to the cloud. We can't find direction for our lives, nor can we hear the voice of the Spirit if we are not positioned under His covering.

Without question, you can find yourself in major trouble if you're wandering in the wilderness and the cloud is nowhere to be seen. But if the cloud is there, just hang on. God has you right where you need to be.

Israel wasn't taken by a direct route to the Promised Land. And it wasn't long before they found themselves in a serious predicament. Behind them—closing fast—was the army of the Egyptians, led by Pharaoh. On either side was the wilderness. Directly in front, blocking their path, was the Red Sea. Suddenly, they were brought to a screeching halt—*Standing At the Edge of the Water.*

OVERCOME WITH FEAR

There are countless people who find themselves at the same place as Israel in our story. Like Israel, they've been released from sin. They have been set free from Egypt—but Pharaoh is doing everything in his power to pull them back into bondage. All they can see in front of them is an imposing obstacle.

Israel had escaped from Pharaoh. But on this side of the Red Sea, God's chosen people weren't completely free from the influence, cruelty, and power of Egypt. As long as they stayed where they were, Israel was trapped, vulnerable, and an easy target. On this side of the Red Sea, they could be easily overtaken, recaptured, and returned to their former slavery.

At that moment, Israel wasn't a nation of warriors. It was a nation of slaves—demoralized bricklayers—who were no match for Pharaoh's army any more than we are a match for the adversities that continue to rise up against us.

No wonder they were afraid. Egypt, a well-oiled military machine, was coming after them, sealing off their retreat. Escape, either to the left or to the right, was prohibited by the wilderness. The sea in front was too large, too perilous to cross. Fear had taken hold. "How can we get our flocks, herds, and families across! If they don't kill us here on the banks of the sea, they will take us back and our task-masters will be harsher than before. Our slavery will be far worse because we'll remember that we were so very close to freedom, but didn't quite make it."

Every time things began to get difficult, Israel grumbled and complained. They talked about the life they had back in Egypt, but they could only remember from a warped perception the good things about their former existence.

19

They longed for the leeks and the garlic and the onions. Their taste buds craved Egyptian salad—all while they were eating angel bread...Manna.

But in the midst of their nostalgia they forgot:

- How they were forced to get up before the break of day.
- How every muscle in their bodies ached as they toiled under the desert sun.
- How their backs were savagely beaten with whips.
- How every time a woman gave birth to a baby, someone came and took that child and threw it to the crocodiles in the Nile River.

Like Israel, too many have forgotten what it was like being a slave to sin. They remember the laughter and the party, but they've blocked the memory of being so drunk they couldn't recall anything that happened the night before; so sick they couldn't do anything but lay in their own vomit. They remember the euphoric high, but they've edited out the part where they spent every last dime they could lay their hands on and stole anything of value so they could get a temporary fix to stop the shaking, chills, and the mental torment.

- They've forgotten the lies they hid behind.
- They've repressed the memory of the sleepless nights when they lay awake, afraid to close their eyes for fear they would never open them again.
- They've forgotten the lack of peace and contentment.
- They've buried the feelings of emptiness, loneliness, and utter helplessness.

Not only did they forget where they came from—but they

failed to remember what their ultimate destination was going to be if they remained in that mess. Why would anyone go back to Egypt? Why would you long to return to the slavery of sin?

Perhaps you've come to this same place multiple times— *Standing At the Edge of the Water.* You've looked at the obstacle in your way and cried, "I've just got to surrender and go back. I can't get across."

I talk with people all the time who keep returning to the same situation over and over in their spiritual walk. They get to a certain spot and are confronted by a barrier that seems insurmountable. Many have trekked this path so many times they grow weary and frustrated. Some have even become afraid to try and move on with God's plan for their lives because they just know they're going to slam into the same wall they've hit every other time.

What you need to know is that God has purposely planned this place you find yourself in right now. The Lord has orchestrated THIS time and THIS place to bring you to full and complete deliverance.

Perhaps all you can see at this moment is an obstacle:

- An advancing army of unpaid bills ready to destroy you.
- A landslide of unresolved conflicts ready to overwhelm your life.
- A tsunami of broken relationships, shattered dreams, squandered potential, and unrealized possibilities, all ready to drag you under.

You may feel you've run out of options, but it's too soon to give up on God. What you fail to understand is that where you presently are is part of your heavenly Father's divine plan to bring such a definitive deliverance to your life that you will

21

never have to worry about being brought back into bondage again.

The trouble you're now facing isn't an accident. It's a situation designed by God just for you. He has led you here.

- You may be in the wilderness—but you're still under His cloud.
- You may feel like you're defeated—but you're still under His cloud.
- You may want to quit—but you're still under His cloud.

This isn't a dead end of defeat or capitulation.

It may be an uncomfortable, fearful spot to be in, but God is going to bring you through!

DARE TO MOVE FORWARD

Even now, as you are reading these words, the Lord is opening a path through the midst of the water. He is once and for all putting an end to the devices of the enemy against your soul. He's releasing His power, bringing you through the water of deliverance and setting you free. You are going to the other side!

When you've safely crossed over, He is going to close in on the forces that have hounded you; those agents of the adversary that have tried to steal, kill, and destroy. On the other shore, you're going to look back and see that the horse and the rider of the enemy have been thrown into the sea. And you're going to sing a song of praise...a song of victory...a song of triumph unto the Lord your God!

His promise is still true: *"When you pass through the*

waters, I will be with you; and through the rivers, they will not overflow you. When you walk through the fire, you will not be burned, nor shall the flame scorch you. For I am the Lord your God, the Holy One of Israel, your Savior" (Isaiah 43:2-3).

Look once again at the words which the Lord spoke through Moses to His people in Exodus 14:13. Don't just read it as part of a story from history, receive it by faith, as God's promise to you today. Moses said to the people (and to you), *"Do not fear. Stand by and see the salvation of the Lord which He will accomplish for you today; for the Egyptians whom you have seen today, you will never see them again forever."*

Claim verse 14: *"The Lord will fight for you while you keep silent."* Pay attention to verse 15: *"Then the Lord said to Moses, 'Why are you crying out to Me? Tell the sons of Israel to go forward.'"*

This is the awesome promise of God for your life—the place to which the Lord is bringing you:

- It's a place of moving forward.
- It's a place of daring to trust God.
- It's a place of believing the Lord is able and willing to bring about your complete deliverance.

Never give up. Never think of retreating. Move forward!

- If you'll dare to move forward – He will break the power of that addiction.
- If you'll dare to move forward – He will break the power of the spirit that's been tormenting your mind.
- If you'll dare to move forward – He will break the power of paralyzing fear.

23

- If you'll dare to move forward – He will break the power of those memories from your past that continue to handicap your walk in the freedom of the Lord.
- If you'll dare to move forward – He will break the power of guilt that haunts you.
- If you'll dare to move forward – He will break the power of discouragement and will open up a fountain of unspeakable joy that will be your strength even in the midst of tough times.

If you'll dare to move forward with faith in Him—no matter the nature of your bondage—He will deliver you! You're *Standing At the Edge of the Water*—but hear the Spirit speaking to your heart, saying, "Come on through."

Complete deliverance is waiting for you, just on the other side.

CHAPTER 2

THE WATER OF BLESSING

The letter arrived in the morning mail. Hurrying back to my office I tore open the envelope and stood reading the answer to the next step in the pursuit of my dream. "Congratulations! You've been accepted into the Master's Program…we look forward to seeing you in the fall."

Music was my passion. I was particularly drawn to accompanying and conducting. Now years of study and hours upon hours in the practice room were being rewarded with an opportunity to further my training and prepare for a bright future and a promising career.

Then, in the midst of celebrating, I heard it. Not an audible voice—but a voice deep within that I had learned to recognize after many years of fellowship and service. It wasn't angry or harsh, yet it was strong and firm, saying, "You can't go."

It seemed that time stood still as I waited, hoping it was the Lord's attempt at humor; wondering if I'd heard correctly, yet all the time knowing I had. Once again He spoke —compassionately, gently, but firmly, repeating, "You can't go."

In that moment, all my dreams, plans, goals, and aspirations were stripped away. I suppose I could have insisted on pursuing my plans, but knew if I did I would go without divine favor and blessing on my life. I reached behind me and dropped the acceptance letter in the trash. I had no idea what the future held. I simply trusted that God had a better plan for my life than anything I could put together on my own.

I don't know if you're aware of it or not, but God has a blessing custom-designed for your life. But in order to bring you into that blessing, He first of all is going to orchestrate a set of circumstances in which you will be stripped and emptied. Only then can He fill you with Himself. That's what we see happening in the life of the man who is the central character of this profound story from the Old Testament (Genesis 32:22-32).

THE DECEIVER

Jacob was one of two brothers—twins—born to Isaac, who was the son of Abraham, and Isaac's wife, Rebecca. Jacob was the second born of the twins and his barely-older brother's name was Esau.

On the day of his birth, Jacob came into the world right behind his brother; so close, in fact, that the Bible records he came out holding onto the heel of his brother, Esau. For that reason they named him Jacob, which means *one who takes by the heel*, or more specifically, *one who supplants*. His name means *deceiver*.

According to the custom of the day, Esau, as the first-born, was the son who was destined to inherit the larger portion of his father's wealth and estate. It was through him that the family name was to be continued. He was to receive the portion designated as the birthright.

However, as the Bible tells us, Esau, who was a hunter, came home one afternoon from the field—and he was hot, tired, and hungry. His brother, Jacob, who was a homebody, was in the tent cooking one of his special recipes for soup. When Esau smelled the aroma wafting from the pot cooking on the open fire, his taste buds went into overdrive and he started to salivate, begging Jacob for a bowl of soup.

Jacob responded, "I'll give you some on one condition. The price for a bowl of my delicious soup is your birthright." Esau, more interested in satisfying the immediate desire of the flesh than he was in the future implications of the deal, made the bargain.

Later, the time came when their aged father, Isaac, was preparing to pronounce the special blessing upon his children. This significant event was more than a prayer which the father would pray over his children. It was also a declaration of future blessings that had prophetic implications.

In preparation for this important moment, Isaac instructed Esau to go hunting...kill fresh game...prepare the meat...bring it to him...and then he would honor him with the blessing of the first-born.

Esau left to do his father's bidding, but in his absence, Jacob took a kid from the flock and seasoned it with his tasty sauce, just the way his father liked it. He impersonated his brother by dressing in one of Esau's robes, and putting the wool of the kid on the back of his hands and the nape of his neck to simulate the hairiness of his brother. Because of his age, Isaac was nearly blind. So when Jacob entered his tent, pretending to be Esau, Isaac was deceived into thinking he was the firstborn, and Jacob received the blessing intended for his brother.

No sooner had he made his exit than Esau returned from the field, went in to receive the blessing, and the deception of Jacob was discovered. Jacob had bought the birthright which gave him the lion's share of the inheritance; now Jacob had stolen the blessing as well.

There was little for Esau to do except become very angry. So angry, in fact, that he decided to wait until his father died (which wouldn't be very long) and then he was going to kill his brother. However, before that plan could be carried out, Jacob received permission to go to the house of his uncle Laban (his mother's brother) and look for a wife from his kinsmen.

TOILING FOR TRUE LOVE

When you read the story of Jacob, one of the things that leaps out is his ingenuity. If you look at him the way most people think, he's deceptive, manipulative, and cowardly. But there is another way to view him. There are some very positive traits in his life. He's a cunning, resourceful, creative man; a person who isn't afraid of rolling up his sleeves and working hard for what he wants. In many ways he is an individual many of us would admire. If he were alive today, he would no doubt be CEO of a large corporation.

So Jacob travels to the home of his Uncle Laban—and arrives penniless. There, in his uncle's house, he meets the girl of his dreams—his cousin, Rachel—and falls hopelessly, madly in love. He asks his uncle for her hand in marriage. Because he has no resources except a strong body and a willingness to work hard for something he really wants, he agrees to labor for his uncle for seven years in order to obtain Rachel as his wife.

It's really a wonderful story. Jacob toiling all those years, working for the one true love of his life. In fact, Scripture records, *"So Jacob served seven years for Rachel and they seemed to him but a few days because of his love for her"* (Genesis 29:20).

You want romance? There it is.

But as cunning as Jacob was, Uncle Laban wasn't above a little trickery himself. Instead of giving Rachel in marriage, Laban substituted her older sister, Leah, and the ruse wasn't discovered until the next morning after the marriage had been consummated. When Jacob awoke and rolled over to gaze into the eyes of his beloved he found to his dismay that it was Leah resting beside him.

Such was his love for Rachel, however, that he agreed to work yet another seven years. And finally they were married. Following the marriages there were children born—first to Leah...then to Rachel's maid...then to Leah's maid...and finally to Rachel.

All this time Jacob was working for Laban. But with his growing family, he realized he needed to devise a way to build his own fortune. You can read about it in Genesis 20—how he separated solid animals from those that were striped and spotted. When it was his turn to receive spotted animals as his wage he saw to it that the animals mated in such a way that they produced spotted offspring. And when he was to receive striped animals as his wage he made sure that the animals mated in such a way that they produced striped offspring.

Jacob was industrious...hard-working...creative...intelligent...diligent. And he was blessed. He had been marked for blessing by his father—and it seemed that everything to which he put his hand prospered.

But then came the day when Jacob realized he had just about worn out his welcome in the tent of Uncle Laban. He also remembered that he had a birthright inheritance in the land of his father. So he gathered up his belongings and all his household and started the journey to the land of his birth.

In Genesis 32, we find Jacob is on his way back home. And the very first verse of chapter 32 is quite interesting because it tells us, *"Now as Jacob went on his way, the angels*

29

of God met him."

CONSUMED WITH FEAR

Think about that verse in light of the rest of the story. Jacob is returning to his homeland. He knows that he's going to have to face his brother, Esau. The last time he saw him, Esau was ready to kill him. But now Jacob has met with the angels of God...and you would think that after this meeting he would have the courage he needed to proceed. But he doesn't. He's still afraid. And being consumed with fear, he begins to devise another plot that may help him out.

All his life Jacob has come up with one plan after another to help him muddle through. Now that he's about to face Esau, who, for all he knows is still angry with him, he feels he won't stand a chance if it comes down to a fight with his brother. So he concocts a plan that he hopes will appease Esau's rage.

He receives the word that his brother is coming to meet him with 400 of his men. Immediately Jacob forgets about the angelic meeting and starts scheming. He divides his entourage into two groups. He thinks, "Perhaps if Esau attacks one group, then the other will be able to escape."

He makes a plan to send gifts ahead of the two groups of people to try and pacify the wrath of his brother. Then he prays—but he was really just praying that God would bless the plan he had already created.

Late in the evening finds Jacob *Standing At the Edge of the Water.* It's a stream called *Jabbok.* On one side is Jacob and all his household. On the other is Esau, coming to meet him.

Now an interesting thing happens at the ford of this stream. The name *Jabbok* means *emptying*—and it is here that Jacob empties himself of everything he owns; all he has worked his entire life to obtain. Jacob sends his entire household on ahead of him across the stream while he, himself, remains behind.

Across the Jabbok amble his camels, his donkeys, his herds, his flocks. Across the stream go his servants, his wives, his maids, and his eleven children. Everything goes. There is a full emptying of all his possessions. And now Jacob is left alone— *Standing At the Edge of the Water.*

WRESTLING ALL NIGHT

To all appearances Jacob has nothing left, but God knows differently. Everything Jacob has is across the "stream of emptying." But Jacob is still standing at the edge. And until Jacob is emptied of Jacob he can't be full of God. And if he's not full of God, then the Lord can't totally bless him in the manner He has determined.

We read, *"Then Jacob was left alone, and a man* [some versions say an angel or the angel of the Lord] *wrestled with him until daybreak"* (verse 24).

For years when I would read this passage I always thought of it as being a place that teaches us about Jacob's perseverance with God until he finally prevails and gets the blessing he seeks from the Lord. But one day as I was studying and praying through the story, I suddenly realized that the wrestling match isn't Jacob's idea at all. Jacob isn't looking for a fight. He isn't looking for a special blessing from God. He isn't struggling with the Lord for an impartation of divine favor. This isn't part of Jacob's plan. As far as he's concerned, he has everything he has ever wanted.

Not once did he think, "Okay, here's what I'll do. I will get my possessions and all my children and wives across the river. And then I'll stand here and wait until I can get a hold

31

of the angel and wrestle him down—then God will give me what I want."

That's not the way it happened! Jacob doesn't wrestle with the heavenly messenger. Instead, according to how I read the text, the heavenly messenger wrestles with Jacob. Now that's a tremendous difference!

God intended to pour out His favor on Jacob; to bring to complete fruition the prophetic prayer of blessing that Isaac had prayed over the head of his son. The Lord wanted to establish Jacob as the patriarch over His chosen people. As far as Jacob was concerned he had everything he needed. He had the birthright, his father's prayer of blessing for the first-born—and he had managed to acquire wealth through his craftiness and ingenuity.

What Jacob didn't understand was that with all he possessed, he still didn't have the full measure of everything God intended for him. And he couldn't receive this because even though he had emptied himself of everything he owned, Jacob was still too full of Jacob. And so the heavenly messenger came to wrestle with him until he could bring him to the point of complete emptiness.

All night—until daybreak—they wrestled with each other. Amazingly, after this long grappling match, Jacob still hadn't said, "uncle." Wrestling with an angelic, heavenly messenger ...until sunrise...and he still wouldn't give up. Jacob is still hanging on to Jacob.

Can't you just hear him protesting? "No! I like being Jacob. I won't be anything other than Jacob. I've been this way all my life, ever since I came out of my mother's womb. Look at all I've been able to do since I've been Jacob. Can't you see everything I've accomplished being myself?"

As the heavenly being wrestles with him, he asks Jacob, "Do you give up? Do you give up?"

"NO! I don't. Why would I? I like the way things are. I like me just as I am. If God will only bless this one small plan I've put together, everything's going to be smoothed out between my brother and me and we will be okay."

Next we read, *"And when he* [the heavenly messenger] *saw that he had not prevailed against him* [Jacob], *he touched the socket of his thigh; so the socket of Jacob's thigh was dislocated [withered] while he wrestled with him"* (verse 25).

Then the angel said, "Let me go." Notice it's not when Jacob saw he had not triumphed over the heavenly messenger. Instead, it's when the heavenly being saw that he had not overcome Jacob—that's when he pleaded, "Now let me go."

The picture I have in mind is of Jacob—*Standing At the Edge of the Water*—when suddenly a guy taps him on the shoulder. Just as he turns around the guy grabs him in a hammer lock and starts throwing him to the floor. Jacob is caught completely by surprise. And the messenger asks, "Do you give up?" And Jacob replies, "No way!"

They toss and tumble. All this time Jacob is trying to get out of the hold of this angelic being.

WHO WILL PREVAIL?

This scene reminds me of watching Saturday morning cartoons as a child. Two guys are fighting and all you see is a swirling cloud of dust with an occasional hand reaching out and then getting pulled back in. In the midst of the melee, one of the combatants tries to crawl off, only to get yanked back into the fray. So it is that every time Jacob breaks free and thinks he's going to run away, the guy reaches out, grabs him, snatches him back, and throws him back down on the ground.

"Do you give? Say uncle!"

"NO! I'm not going to give up!"

They keep going. Jacob breaks free and runs off. He grabs him again...and throws him down once more. All night this continues. And the angel can't prevail over Jacob because he is just too stubborn and self-willed.

Finally the guy sees that dawn is breaking. He needs to leave. He has been on earth long enough and has tried every hold he knows. He's used every routine he has—and nothing causes Jacob to surrender. He then decides, "I'm just going to have to hurt him."

The messenger always had the power to do what was necessary, but it's almost as if he's been trying to work with him in such a way that he won't really need to be injured. It reminds me of fathers and sons playing at wrestling. Sometimes fathers come out on the bad end of that deal, but the dad is usually thinking, "I've got to pull my punches. I have to be careful so I don't injure the little fellow."

The angel is trying to get Jacob to concede—but he refuses. Finally he says, "All right, I've got to get out of here. The sun is rising. I guess I am just going to have to hurt him." And he touches him on the hip...and it dislocates.

HE WOULDN'T LET GO!

Suddenly, everything changes. Because when Jacob is hurt, there is an immediate revelation. "I'm battling something I didn't even know I was wrestling with. I'm struggling with a power so much greater than anything I ever knew. I am wrestling with—the ANGEL of the Lord."

Later on he says, "I've seen the face of God."

It finally dawned on Jacob, "I'm wrestling with the manifest presence of Glory! And He—Oh wow!—He can take me anytime He wants."

Until this moment, the heavenly messenger had held onto Jacob and asked, "Will you give up?" But now the messenger is trying to leave because dawn is breaking. The revelation of who he's been battling causes Jacob to panic. Even in his injured state, he grabs *him* and says, "NO! You can't get away from me! I'm not going to let you leave until you bless me, because now I have come to the end of myself and see my full expression of weakness. Now I understand that nothing in me is good. I've got to have your help. I'm not turning you loose. You can struggle all you want, but I am not letting go until you bless me. I've GOT to have the blessing!"

God had to bring Jacob to the point of brokenness before he realized his absolute dependence upon the Lord and his need for divine blessing. Once his hip was dislocated, he was determined to not let go until he had been blessed. Now Jacob isn't wrestling in order to hang onto Jacob; he is wrestling in order to hang onto God.

Before, it was the heavenly messenger holding onto Jacob...and Jacob was trying to get away, attempting to hang onto Jacob. But the tables have turned, and it's Jacob clinging to the messenger, who is trying to break away, but Jacob is latching on for all he's worth because he has come to the end of himself and realizes his resources aren't enough. He understands he needs God's help—the Lord's divine blessing. He's not going to let go—because he is desperate for God.

When Jacob has emptied himself not only of all that he has, but also of all that he is—that's when God sees that he has changed and pours out His favor. And the great transformation is marked by giving him a new name.

No longer is he Jacob—heel-grabber...supplanter... deceiver. He is now Israel—a prince...one who wrestles with God and prevails...one who has the strength of God as his help.

Notice verse 27 where the heavenly messenger says to him, *"What is your name? And he said, 'Jacob.'"*

Before God can truly change him, Jacob first has to

acknowledge who he really is. He has to admit that he is a deceiver...supplanter...one who gets by on his ingenuity...a person who has made it through his own cunning.

Only when Jacob confesses his true nature and empties out his reliance upon the flesh can the Lord truly change and bless him.

The rest of the story is found in subsequent chapters. In them you learn that there is peace between the brothers. You read of the prosperity of Jacob—now known as Israel. You discover the beginnings of a mighty nation—the chosen, blessed people of God. But there is always a reminder of this day when Jacob found himself *Standing At the Edge of the Water.* Verse 31 tells us about this when it says, *"Now the sun rose upon him just as he crossed over Penuel, and he was limping on his thigh."*

Jacob was blessed of God—but he walked with a limp. Through the rest of his days, even though he was highly favored and divinely blessed, he carried a permanent reminder of the time when he was at the water's edge...the place where he wrestled until "self" was gone. And the water of emptying became for him the water of blessing.

EMPTY YOURSELF OF YOU

Chapter 11 of the New Testament Book of Hebrews contains what is known as the Faith Hall of Fame. In verse 21 of that chapter we are told, *"By faith Jacob, as he was dying, blessed each of the sons of Joseph, and worshiped, leaning on the top of his staff."*

In his old age, Jacob is passing on the blessing of God to his grandchildren. As he worships the Lord—he is leaning on the top of his staff.

The reason he is doing this is not because he's old; it is

because he walks with a limp, still carrying the reminder of the time at that brook when God touched him.

As you've been reading the story of this man, perhaps you can identify with him. At the very beginning of this chapter I told you God has a specific blessing custom-designed for your life. It has your name on it. He has a special mark of divine favor that He wants to place upon your forehead.

Perhaps you've prayed for God's help in a particular area for a very long time. But while you've prayed, you've been scheming, planning, working, and exercising all your options—trying every avenue you knew to bring it to pass. You may have even been pretty successful at it.

But God is trying to elevate you to another level. He desires to bring you into a new dimension of His power, love, grace, mercy, and abundant blessing—something that is beyond your wildest imagination.

You no doubt already understand the concept of surrender—emptying. You fully grasp the significance of placing everything across the Jabbok. You've probably already done that. There's no question that the Lord can call for anything you have at any moment and you'll relinquish it to Him.

But the Lord has you at the water's edge. And it's not your possessions that He's trying to get across the stream of emptying. It's YOU.

God has a special place into which He's trying to bring you. But it's going to require both a name and a character change—and a new way of thinking about and perceiving your life. God's trying to get you to empty yourself of YOU so that you can then be truly filled with Him.

Yes, it's a wrestling match—because you've lived with yourself for so long. There are things you're not proud of, but you have grown comfortable with them and learned how to deal with their presence. But the truth is you can't hang onto them and receive the blessings of God which He wants to bring to your life.

It isn't just negative stuff you're going to have to release. It may be something in you that's good and admirable that has to go. God doesn't work through your self-styled goodness—because if He did, then it wouldn't be clear where His blessing stopped and your ingenuity began.

So here you are—*Standing At the Edge of the Water.* The place of emptying. The place of admitting your own initiative has failed and your human ability won't carry you to the next level. You find yourself wrestling with God.

The Spirit of the Lord is speaking to your heart, asking, "Do you give up?" Not your *stuff*—YOU! And the things that make you who you are. Are you willing to give everything up for Him?

God has targeted you for His blessing. So don't hang on in stubborn resistance until He has to bring you to the place of brokenness in order for you to realize your desperate need. Surrender yourself to the Lord so He can pour out His favor on your life—starting today.

CHAPTER 3

THE WATER OF PROMISE

Moses is dead. He led the children of Israel out of Egyptian bondage and shepherded them through the wilderness for 40 years. He performed miracles and was the mouthpiece of God to His people. He was the only leader some of them had ever known. But now he's gone. And his protégé, Joshua has been appointed to take his place.

As Joshua assumes his role of leadership, he and all of Israel are *Standing At the Edge of the Water.* It's the Jordan River—the dividing line between the wilderness and the land of Canaan. On one side are all the memories and hardships of the wilderness wandering. Just across the river lies the land of blessing God has promised as the inheritance for the people of Israel.

Joshua and the Israelites are on the banks of the Jordan— the water of PROMISE (Joshua 3:1-17).

You will remember that this isn't the first time Israel has prepared to enter the Promised Land. Forty years earlier, they stood at the boundary of Canaan—fresh out of being delivered from the bondage of Egypt. Moses was their leader, Aaron was their priest, and Joshua was just a young man.

In preparation for their conquest of Canaan, Moses commissioned 12 leaders—one from each of the tribes of Israel—to carry out a reconnaissance mission. For 40 days the men explored the territory from just above Kadesh-barnea in the south to Rehob, a city at the northern end of the Jordan valley, near Mount Hermon. When the 12 spies returned, they gave their report to Moses and the people.

As part of their presentation, they displayed some of the produce of the land. Figs. Pomegranates. Grape clusters from the Valley of Eshcol so big it took two men to carry them suspended on a pole. This territory was fertile and prosperous—they described its abundance by calling it a land flowing with milk and honey.

That was the good news. But while they were detailing all the bounty of the Promised Land there were ten men who had something else on their minds. Yes, it was true that Canaan was a place of prosperity and plenty, but the inhabitants were fierce warriors. There were walled cities built like fortresses that seemed impregnable. There were giants. The fear of what they had witnessed was evident on their faces and in their words. When they compared themselves to the men of Canaan, they seemed like grasshoppers in their own eyes (see Numbers 13).

Twelve men were sent to spy out the land:

- Ten men returned with a negative report.
- Ten men returned feeling like grasshoppers.
- Ten men returned feeling defeated before they even began.
- Ten men returned discouraged...filled with doubt and fear.

However, there were two individuals who came back with a glowing report and exclaimed, "The land is wonderful and fertile; everything we hoped it would be and more. Yes, there are fortified cities and there are giant warriors. But our God has assured us that this is ours for the taking—and we have confidence in the promises of our God."

Ten men were so fearful of the giants they couldn't believe what God had guaranteed. Two men were so convinced of the Lord's promise that nothing could shake their faith, not even a few giants.

As usually happens, the majority report carried the day. But this account illustrates how the majority isn't always right. In this instance they were wrong—dead wrong. They were so wrong that Israel was sentenced to roaming in the wilderness for 40 years until every person 20 years old and up at the time died, and a new generation had been raised up. The only exception was the two men who brought back a positive report of faith—Joshua and Caleb.

FOLLOW, FUNCTION, FOCUS

Fast forward 40 years. The wilderness wandering is over. Joshua is the leader—and he's once again preparing for the conquest of Canaan. He's *Standing At the Edge of the Water*—the water of PROMISE. Just across the river lies everything that has been promised by Almighty God. All that stands between Israel and Canaan is Jordan.

Now, to the casual observer, it would appear that God had brought Israel to this place at the wrong time of the year. It was the season when the snows were melting in the mountains and the streams were feeding into the Jordan, causing it to overflow its banks. This was no longer a gentle flowing body of water—it was a swollen, rushing current.

There was no shallow area to ford the river, no ferry to carry them across, and no suspension bridge to span. It seemed like the logical thing to do would be to wait until a better, more advantageous season.

But just when it looked like they were going to have to

camp for an extended period beside the river, God told them, "Now is the time. Tell the people to get ready...and move out. This is the time to press forward into the land of blessing. This is the time to receive the promise I have made to you."

Amazing! What seems to be the most unlikely, illogical season, is when God says, "Move forward."

In obedience Joshua stood before the people and announced, "Prepare yourselves. When I give the signal, move forward." And then he added something that is both simple and profound: *"You have not passed this way before"* (Joshua 3:4).

When you read the story you discover that the Lord gave some very specific instructions to follow so that they could cross the Jordan and possess the promise. These steps become a prescription for us today if we are going to be a partaker of the blessings of God which have been pledged to us.

FOLLOW THE PLAN

When God told Joshua to lead the people across the Jordan, He gave him a plan of action. The priests were to take the Ark of the Covenant—which was the visible symbol of the presence of God—out of the tabernacle. They were to place it on their shoulders, carry it to the Jordan River, step into the river, and then the waters were going to be rolled back so that Israel could cross over into Canaan.

That was the directive, but I'm sure there were some skeptics in the crowd. After all, the nation of Israel wrote the procedural manual for miraculously crossing bodies of water. It was written in their record books. If your objective is to move a nation across a span of water there were steps to follow:

- Step one: have the leader pick up his staff.
- Step two: hold the staff out over the water.
- Step three: God responds and sends a wind to blow a path through the water.
- Step four: the river bed dries up.
- Step five: the nation walks across on dry ground with a wall of water on either side of them.

That's the way it was done before—it says so right here in the manual. There had been a practice run at the Red Sea 40 years earlier. Nothing was written down about the Ark of the Covenant, the priests, or anything referring to walking into the water before it parts. Not a word was mentioned about the priests getting their feet wet.

I can hear them questioning, "God, are you sure this is YOUR plan? We've never done it this way before."

The answer came back loud and clear: "No, you've not seen it done like this in times past, but you've never been this way before either." A new path requires a new plan.

This isn't Moses—it's a new leader, Joshua. This isn't the Red Sea—it is a new place, the Jordan. This isn't deliverance OUT of bondage—this is bringing you INTO the promise.

Where are you on your journey today? Perhaps you are sensing the Spirit of the Lord moving you into a new place, a new day, a new season. Maybe He's leading you out of what you've always known; your comfort zone. You have spent too long in the wilderness, and now you feel the Lord moving you toward the fulfillment of promise in your life. Yet, you are hesitant because you've never been this way before.

What do you hear God saying to you? How is He leading? Remember, His words: *"For My thoughts are not your thoughts, nor are your ways My ways...For as the heavens are higher than the earth, so are My ways higher than your ways and My thoughts than your thoughts"* (Isaiah 55:8-9).

You would never in a million years do it this way—but all indicators are pointing to a fresh, seemingly impossible approach. No matter how unfamiliar it seems to a logical mind, when God speaks, put your own thoughts aside and *follow the plan!*

FUNCTION IN FAITH

It required a great deal of faith for the priests carrying the Ark of the Covenant to step into the raging current of the Jordan. It took total belief and trust for the nation of Israel to walk through the river bed and attempt to possess the land of Canaan. Just because God had promised this territory to His people didn't mean there wouldn't be any resistance to them settling there. Indeed, there were great obstacles to overcome. The giants hadn't moved. And in order for Israel to inherit the promise, they had to deal with the adversary.

When they became fearful and ran from the enemy 40 years prior, it cost them dearly. But when they trusted the word of the Lord and moved forward in obedience to Him, the walls collapsed, the giants were defeated, and they obtained the promise.

The moment you determine that the Lord is going to be first in your life, purpose to press into the things of God, decide to obediently follow His plan, and embrace the promises of your heavenly father, be assured a spiritual attack will be launched against you that will range from minor distractions to a major calamity.

None of us inherit the place of promise without a struggle—without removing the strongholds and defeating the giants of self-will, envy, comparing ourselves with others, unforgiveness, bitterness, the fear of failure, and rejection. In addition, we're going to have to tear down perhaps the largest stronghold of all—pride.

The reason Israel failed to enter Canaan the first time was

because of unbelief born of fear. That's why in Joshua 1, when the Lord begins to speak to His servant about going in to possess the promised land, He tells Joshua over and over again not to be afraid.

Perhaps at this very moment you are facing head-on, some serious issues. Maybe you're looking at how things are going—and you've never taken this route before. The idea of something this strange, new, different, and challenging is causing you sleepless nights and anxious days.

If the odds seem overwhelming, remember, your God specializes in things thought impossible.

Hear the word of the Lord:

- *"Be strong and courageous"* (Joshua 1:6).
- *"Be strong and very courageous; be careful to do according to all the law...do not turn from it to the right or to the left, so that you may have success wherever you go"* (verse 7).
- *"Be strong and courageous! Do not tremble or be dismayed, for the Lord your God is with you wherever you go"* (verse 9).

It's possible that you are *Standing At the Edge of the Water*—and it is a rushing current that has overflowed its banks. You may not have any idea how you're going to get across to possess the promise of God for your life. In fact, you may be on the verge of giving up, thinking this kind of thing is good for other people, but it just doesn't seem to work for you.

Rest assured that God has a plan. He doesn't make promises just to tantalize you without providing a way of helping you receive them. You've never been this way before, or had to believe and rely on the Lord to such an extent. In the past there has always been somebody else to lean on, but they can't help you now. This is a new path. Take courage in the knowledge that the Lord is going before you!

Today, face your fears and permit faith to rise in your heart as you step into the water. You're not alone—God is with you and is preparing the way. He is *not* going to leave you to wander in the wilderness. He is *not* going to let you drown in the Jordan. But He *is* going to see to it that you are brought safely into the land of promise and blessing that He has prepared.

So follow the plan, function in faith, and get ready to take the third step:

FOCUS ON THE LORD

Just before it was time to cross the Jordan, Joshua's men spread this word to all the camps, *"When you see the ark of the covenant of the Lord your God with the Levitical priests carrying it, then you shall set out from your place and go after it"* (Joshua3:3).

All the tribes of Israel were to have an unrestricted view of the Ark, which was the symbol of the presence of God:

- As they focused on the Ark they would know which direction to travel.
- As they focused on the Ark they would remember the power of God that was working on their behalf.
- As they focused on the Ark it would be a reminder that the Lord had made a covenant with His people which He would not break.

I want to remind you that you're serving a God who has made a covenant with you through His only begotten Son, Jesus Christ. If you want to overcome any obstacle and step over into the land of promise—the place of His divine presence—you must keep before you a clear view of the Lord Jesus Christ who has pledged to never leave you or forsake you, but to be by your side to the end of the age.

No matter the barrier—Christ has already gone before you. While you have never walked this path before—He has!

One day the Lord Jesus went to the Garden of Gethsemane to pray. There, the waters of turmoil rolled in front of Him as a river that seemingly could not be forded.

Then, He was nailed to a cross on a hill called Calvary. And it looked as if the waters would surely overtake Him.

Finally, Christ died and they laid Him in a tomb and sealed it with a huge stone over the entrance. It seemed like the waters of death had completely overwhelmed Him.

But early on the morning of the first day of the week, He proved that the cross and the tomb were not the end—but only the beginning. He arose in glory. He spoiled principalities and powers and made a public show of their weakness. They were conquered by His resurrection.

Jesus Christ has already triumphed. He has gone before you. He has stepped into the water ahead of you and by His power has cleared a path for you to walk. He rose in victory, spoiled the enemy, and repulsed every attack of Satan. He is our conquering King.

To everyone who passes through the water; to those who fix their gaze upon Him and follow in His footsteps, He promises, "I will be with you...wherever you go."

As you keep your eyes on Jesus, victory is yours—over every temptation, over every evil way, over every yoke of bondage.

THE WATERS ARE ROLLED BACK!

One of the biggest reasons we can't get past the obstacles

in our lives is because we spend our time dwelling on the circumstances—instead of Jesus. We pray so hard for help with our problem, and try everything we know to overcome it. For many, their entire walk with the Lord seems to be centered on getting past some particular issue.

The answer is to simply become consumed with God's Son. Seek Him. Focus on Him. Follow Him. Trust Him, and be filled with His presence. Instead of telling Jesus how big your problem is—start telling your problem how big your Jesus is!

When a child of God turns his eyes to the Lord Jesus, then between the impossibility and self, there HE is. After such a life-changing encounter, the person no longer talks about "getting the victory." It isn't the victory he wants—it is the Victor. He doesn't speak of "striving for a new blessing" and "seeking to enter a new experience." His eyes are fixed on the Lord Jesus. He puts Christ between himself and the onslaught of the devil. And he looks up into His face—and there IS victory.

Perhaps you're *Standing At the Edge of the Water*—and it's the water of PROMISE. You are ready to go a direction you have never been before...to possess the promises of God and experience the Lord's presence and power at work in your life to the praise of His glory.

Remember: Follow the plan. Function in faith. Focus on the Lord.

He has already stepped into the water—and the Jordan won't keep you away any longer. It's already rolled back. The Master is inviting you across into the place He has promised; the place of divine blessing and favor.

CHAPTER 4

THE WATER OF PROVISION

BAM! What sounded like a minor explosion from the front end of the car awakened me with a jolt from a sound sleep in the back seat. Opening my eyes I could see smoke pouring from under the hood and the most horrible banging rose above the sounds of the thunderstorm through which we were driving. It sounded like the engine was going to drop out at any moment!

Dad was at the wheel and he immediately pulled over and brought the car to a stop. In the pouring rain he got out, raised the hood, and tried to find the problem. After a few minutes he climbed back into the car, but the only thing to show for his efforts was his now-drenched clothing. Dad would never take a major highway when he could drive a deserted country road as an alternate route, and tonight was no exception. There was nobody on this middle-of-nowhere road during this storm.

Hoping to get to a place where we could find some help Dad turned the key in the ignition, but the engine was silent. As a young boy, I always thought my father could handle anything, but on this occasion I saw—perhaps for the first time—his helplessness.

I will never forget as Dad bent his head over the steering wheel and prayed. He reminded the Lord how he had preached that very night about the sufficiency of His grace. Now he was on his way home with his family, tired, with no resources, a broken down vehicle, and no evidence of civilization for miles. He called on the Lord for help. Then he straightened up, once more turned the key—and with a cough and a sputter, the engine started.

For the rest of the journey we could only drive about 35 miles per hour or the car would shake and sound like it was literally falling apart. Finally, in the wee hours of the morning, we arrived safely home.

The next day Dad managed to start the car and drive to the repair shop. He stopped just outside the service bay, went inside and explained what had happened. When the mechanic asked him to drive the vehicle into the service area, Dad turned the key in the ignition and the engine completely froze. Later we discovered that a piston had broken in half and had just been knocking back and forth for the entire time we were making our way home. Miraculously, it hadn't jammed in the engine block for over 100 miles!

God's grace had indeed been sufficient. Just when we needed Him most, He provided. It wasn't opulence, but it was sustenance.

AN ANSWER IN THE DARKEST OF DAYS

Have you ever been in a situation where you were earnestly trying to accomplish all that God asked you to do, yet, no matter how hard you tried, or how much energy you exerted, it seemed like things were getting harder and harder just to survive? Then, when you didn't think you could possibly take any more, the only avenue of help and resource closed down. The single thread to which you were clinging was suddenly clipped. Ever been there?

If you have, then you can relate to the prophet Elijah in

this episode from the chronicles of the people of Israel (1 Kings 17:1-16).

In the New Testament book of James, chapter 5, there is an interesting statement that says, *"Elijah was a man with a nature like ours..."* (verse 17).

As we look at the following story it's important to keep that in mind, because all too often when we read about the lives of people in the Bible we have this tendency to separate them from the real world. In Scripture they often appear larger than life and seem to be somehow untouchable —always getting it right in the end...and never really struggling in-between.

It's noteworthy to remember that the prophet Elijah wasn't a super saint. He wasn't from another planet and couldn't leap tall buildings in a single bound. Bullets didn't bounce off his chest. He was a man with a human nature —just like ours.

GOD'S MAN OF FAITH AND POWER

Not a great deal is known about the origins and background of Elijah. He suddenly bursts on the scene as a man sent from God right in the midst of some of the darkest days in the Northern Kingdom of Israel.

Ahab is the ruling king, and under his reign Israel sank to her lowest place in the eyes of God: the word of the Lord was rejected, and the God of Israel was replaced with worship of the heathen gods, Baal and Asherah. Scripture dismisses the entire rule of King Ahab by telling us, *"Thus Ahab did more to provoke the Lord God of Israel than all the kings of Israel who were before him"* (1 Kings 16:33).

Into this reign of evil rejection of God, Elijah the Tishbite suddenly appears as the prophet of the Lord with a message for the king that God is going to withhold rain from the land until Elijah gives the command for it to rain again.

The challenge which the prophet flung in Ahab's face wasn't only a rebuke of his evil conduct, but it was also an outright attack upon the power of the false god, Baal. This pagan god of the Canaanites was sometimes called the "storm god." He was the one who allegedly brought rain, showers, mist, and dew to the parched land. It was supposedly in the authority of Baal to provide the abundance which guaranteed fertility—fertility of the fields, the flocks, and even among the people who worshiped him.

With his pronouncement, Elijah challenged the power of Baal to produce any rain, at any time, anywhere. According to his prophetic word, there would be a devastating drought as proof positive that this pagan deity was a sham created by the fantasy of man.

Just as suddenly as Elijah appears—he disappears.

- Just when it looked like there was going to be a showdown...
- Just when it seemed Elijah was on the scene to stay and to call the nation back to the worship of the one true God...
- Just when it appeared that Jehovah was going to once more be exalted in the land...

The Lord instructed Elijah to go underground.

MIRACLES AT THE BROOK

Remember that Elijah had a nature like you and me. His was a fiery temperament. As such, he would no doubt have preferred to remain in the public eye, but that wasn't God's intention. The Lord knew that the timing of the battle was as important as the conflict itself. So God sent Elijah into hiding.

The seasonal rains didn't arrive. The land was cracked, parched and dry; the crops didn't grow; food was becoming increasingly scarce. Keeping body and soul together was more than a full-time job. But God had a plan for preserving His servant.

The Lord instructed Elijah to travel east and hide by the brook, Cherith. There, by that small stream, God provided for the prophet in the midst of severe drought and famine. The Bible tells us that the Lord commanded ravens to bring him food. And with the water from the brook and the food from the ravens, Elijah was sustained.

Understand that this brook, Cherith, wasn't the babbling, singing mountain stream of cool, clear water that many people have tried to make it out to be. The name *Cherith* means *the cutting place*—and it was where a small seep of water had worn away the rock and stone. It wasn't crystal clear by any stretch of the imagination. It was a desolate oasis —polluted, both by the desert sand and by the wild animals desperate to quench their thirst.

Not only that, but it wasn't fresh baked loaves of bread and grilled steak which the ravens brought to Elijah every day for food. Ravens are scavenger birds. In the Hebrew tradition, they were regarded as unclean, contaminated, and an abomination because of their foraging habits. The food of ravens was that which was plucked from the carcasses left by the jackals and hyenas of the desert. Any discarded fragments of bad food or rotten wastes that were flung outside the village walls were pounced upon by ravens. This was the food on which Elijah survived.

For some people that's a little hard to imagine because they have been led to believe that life for God's people must always be beautiful and comfortable. But the reality is that in the life of every child of God there will come a cutting place—a Cherith where faith is tested and refined.

The Psalmist sang, *"Many are the afflictions of the righteous..."*(Psalm 34:19) And Jesus Christ Himself declared, *"In the world you will have tribulation..."* (John 16:33 NKJV).

THE CUTTING PLACE

Just because there is a time of testing and refining doesn't necessarily mean that the devil is attacking. Sometimes it is the work of the Lord taking us to the brook, Cherith—taking us to the cutting place. He's trying to bring us to where all of our selfish motives...all of our selfish desires...all of our personal plans and agendas...all of our dependency and allegiances...are cut away until we are left with nothing but God and God alone.

It can be a painful ordeal to do the Father's will—bringing us to a place of humiliation and trying our faith. Just because we have decided to follow the Lord doesn't mean we will be exempt from the trauma of our times. When the economy is in a downturn...when the family is under attack...when society is becoming increasingly secularized...when the crime rate is soaring...when the nation is at war—it affects us all. No one is immune.

The difference between the believer and the person of this world is that the child of God has a sure and certain hope, regardless of what's happening around him. Even in the midst of traumatic days we have the assurance of the Lord that He will see us through. It may not be opulence, but it will be sustenance.

As sons and daughters of our heavenly Father, we have the promise that this present world is not all there is. This life is not the be-all and the end-all. There is a better day ahead, and glory is at the end of the journey. We're not going to get the real reward in this life; that will take place when we stand in His eternal presence, washed in the blood of the Lamb, clothed in the righteous robe of Jesus Christ, and the Father looks at us, extends His hand, and welcomes us into His presence. When He says, "Well done, good and faithful servant. You have been faithful over a few things, I'm going to make you ruler over many things. Enter into the joys of the Lord"—*That's* when we get our real reward!

So here we find Elijah and he is *Standing At the Edge of the Water*—and it's the water of PROVISION. I'm certain this isn't really what he had in mind when he pictured God providing for him. He didn't envision the cutting place, the brook, Cherith.

There are two things the Lord is trying to accomplish in him. They are also what God is seeking to achieve in you and me when He brings us to the cutting place; where our faith is tested and we are stripped of all the excess baggage and unnecessary weights.

First: He is developing TRUST.

- We won't really learn to trust God when everything is going our way.
- We won't learn to trust Him when we laugh and the world laughs with us.
- We won't learn to trust Him when our bank account is bulging, the new automobile is running smoothly, the kids are healthy, and the house is newly furnished.

Trust is learned at the cutting place of testing: when adversity strikes without warning...when all the resources are exhausted...when the fare is meager and the excitement is

55

gone. It is during tough times and in tough places that we learn to trust.

Before Elijah could experience the glorious victory over the prophets of Baal on Mount Carmel where he called fire down from heaven to consume the sacrifice, he had to first learn trust at the brook, Cherith.

In order to ever have what 1 John 5:4 calls, *"the victory that has overcome the world,"* we must first go through the cutting place where our faith is challenged in the crucible of adversity and stretched, pulled, pushed, squeezed, and put through every kind of test imaginable.

When we arrive at that moment of absolute trust:

- We begin to understand that when God is all we have —He is enough!
- We begin to understand that though the afflictions may be many—the Lord delivers us out of them all.
- We begin to understand that even though we may have tribulations in this world, we can be of good cheer—because the Lord Jesus Christ has overcome the world. He is in us and we are in Him. His promise is that in all things we are more than conquerors through Him.

Second: Not only do we learn Trust in the cutting place—but we also develop COMMUNION.

Most of the time we are so preoccupied with life that we don't have time to really commune with God. We have jobs to perform, deadlines to meet, functions to attend, recreation to pursue. And communion with God just gets left out of the mix.

But when the job is gone, when there's no money for recreation, when the phone doesn't ring, and friends have abandoned us—suddenly we find time. It is in the quietness that we can reconnect with the Lord and have communion with the Father. In the stillness we can develop a listening ear that is sensitive to His voice.

I've discovered that the longer we are discontent with our station and the more we complain about being in the cutting place—the longer we have to stay there.

Some of us don't get down to business with God in prayer until trouble strikes. We don't make church attendance a priority until the world starts caving in on us. Many don't really call on the Lord until they've exhausted every other possibility. So God will keep us at Cherith until we have learned the lessons of trust and communion.

The Bible doesn't tell us just how long Elijah was sustained at Cherith, but 1 Kings 17:7 records that after a while, the brook dried up. It wasn't much to begin with, but now there wasn't a drop of water left. Suddenly, the one small resource he depended upon was gone.

I've found that most of us can handle the adversity when there is at least a trickle of supply; some token of help. With just a slim strand of hope, we will hang in there and keep going.

But what happens when the brook dries up?

- When the one thing we could count on is no longer available?
- When the small source of income is taken away?
- When the one friend we could rely on is gone?
- When the robust health we could always depend on is no longer there?

Some see the dried up brook as a sign that the Lord has lost interest in them; that He no longer loves or cares about them. Others begin to question God's power; they begin to doubt He is able to make a difference in their life. Still others question whether or not there really is a God at all.

When the mistrust creeps in, there are those who try different mechanisms to cope. They will cop out, deny the reality of the dried up brook, or try to escape with something that will keep their mind off the fact that their resources are depleted. They will turn to alcohol, drugs, shopping, food—and some even abandon the church and their faith. They react to adversity the way Job's wife encouraged him to respond—to curse God and die. They give up and throw in the towel. They quit!

WHEN THE BROOK RUNS DRY

I may be writing these words to a person whose brook has just dried up. Your last hope, the one thing that was keeping you going, is gone.

You need to know that adversity in your life isn't necessarily a sign of a lack of spirituality. Don't equate the spectacular with the spiritual. God's obvious blessings are not always a sign of His approval, nor does the apparent lack of His favor indicate His disapproval.

Just about the time we start relying on the provision of the brook, God's going to dry it up. The reason is because He doesn't want us depending on the brook—He wants us trusting in Him.

Taking on a second job is not our source. Neither is the one friend who listens to us. Medication isn't our answer, nor is the ability to come up with creative solutions. There's only one true source—and that is the Lord. The moment we start trusting something or someone else more than we trust Him is when that particular brook is going to dry up, because God wants us to remember that He and He alone is our source.

When we are following the Lord in true obedience and have staked our lives to His will and way—when we are His child and He is our Lord—then, when our brook dries up, get ready for something spectacular! God is about to bring His help and supply in such a miraculous way that we would never have thought of it in our wildest imagination.

Right on the heels of the brook drying up, verses 8 and 9 tell us, *"Then the word of the Lord came to him, saying, 'Arise, go to Zarephath, which belongs to Sidon, and stay there; behold, I have commanded a widow there to provide for you.'"*

Elijah started at Cherith—the cutting place. Next God tells him to walk to Zarephath—which means "to smelt, or to melt." The prophet thought the cutting place was bad enough, but now God was sending him to the melting place.

Elijah never dreamed that a widow woman in the midst of the enemies of Israel would be the one through whom God would work a miracle of provision for his life. The melting place is certainly not where he expected to find sustenance. It went against every ounce of conventional wisdom and flew in the face of all he knew and understood.

But when the brook dried up, God had prepared a widow with limited resources who was willing to trust the word of the Lord as spoken by the mouth of the prophet. Through her meager supply, God was not only going to sustain His prophet, but He was going to honor her faith and provide for a widow and her young son until the famine was over.

Picture this. Here is this emaciated prophet—lips dry and cracked, skin flaking, voice barely a croaking whisper—stumbling into the village. He sees the lady gathering a few sticks. She's moving slowly, conserving what little energy she has left. For just a moment their eyes meet and he asks for help—for a drop of water to quench his thirst. Compassion comes naturally to her and she turns to go and find some water for him. Then, with a confidence that belies his condition, he adds, "And please bring me just a morsel of bread to eat."

Any other time she would have automatically extended that gesture of hospitality, but today is different. There's no bread in the house. She was out gathering a few sticks to make what would be her last cooking fire, for all she had left was a handful of meal in the barrel and a little bit of oil in the jar. She had planned to make one last meager meal for herself and her son and then they would crawl off somewhere to die like so many in the village had already done.

But she couldn't ignore this request. There was something about the man who was making it. There was hope in his eyes—even in his gaunt, wasted condition, there was a glimmer of hope. And there was promise in his words: "For *thus says the Lord God of Israel, 'The bowl of flour shall not be exhausted, nor shall the jar of oil be empty, until the day that the Lord sends rain on the face of the earth'"* (verse 14).

Driven by desperation, the widow silenced the inner voices of fear and doubt and responded in obedience to the word of the Lord. She trusted what little she had into the hands of the prophet and, through a source that seemed so unlikely, God provided a daily miracle.

She pulled out the flour, mixed in the oil, cooked the little cake, and brought it to the man of God. He ate it—then told her to go and prepare something for herself and her son. She protested, "I gave you the last of the flour. There's nothing left." But he insisted. And so, to placate him, she went back to the barrel. She reached in her hand—and to her surprise found that there was another handful of flour. She shook the bottle of oil—and out dribbled enough to finish making the meal.

When it came time to eat again, she was certain they

were going to go hungry, but the prophet said, "Go check again." And every day, when it was time to prepare the food, there was always just a small handful of flour and a few drops of oil; enough for one more meal—daily bread.

Day...by day...by day...through the duration of the famine, the Lord provided for the prophet, the widow, and her son through the obedience of a woman who would dare put her trust in the word of the Lord as spoken by the man of God.

AMAZING PROVISION

If your brook has gone dry...if you've exhausted the last of your resources—then get ready. Because God is about to do something wonderful to show Himself mighty on your behalf. He is preparing to send His word with an instruction that will bring a blessing of provision to your life that you won't believe until you actually experience it.

This is the amazing God we serve. He has always provided for His children.

The Creator started in the Book of Genesis with the very first man and woman. Even when they strayed and disobeyed, He provided a covering for them—and it became the means of their redemption.

God took a man named Abraham who was His servant—who obeyed the voice of the Lord and led his son to the top of the mountain to be sacrificed. With his knife extended, ready to take Isaac's life, the Lord had another plan...and a ram was placed on the altar instead. It was there that God gave His covenant name: "I am Jehovah-jireh—the Lord who will provide."

When Israel was wandering in the wilderness God provided water from a rock; He supplied "angel bread" that fell to the ground every morning. Through 40 years of wilderness walking, the Lord caused their shoes not to wear out or their clothes to get holes.

God provided for Daniel. When he was thrown into the lions' den He sent an angel to shut the mouths of the ravenous animals.

He took care of the three Hebrew boys who were cast into the midst of a fiery furnace. When the king looked over into the flame, he exclaimed, *"Did we not cast three men bound into the midst of the fire?...Look!...I see four men loose, walking in the midst of the fire; and they are not hurt, and the form of the fourth is like the Son of God"* (Daniel 3: 24-25 NKJV).

The Lord has always provided for His people. To the believers at Corinth, the Apostle Paul wrote: *"No temptation has overtaken you but such as is common to man; and God is faithful, who will not allow you to be tempted beyond what you are able, but with the temptation will provide the way of escape also, so that you will be able to endure it"* (1 Corinthians 10:13).

Finally, the Almighty gave the ultimate provision for lost humanity when He sent His only begotten Son into the world. When we were without love, hope, and help—our loving heavenly Father sent Jesus.

God will provide! You can trust Him! He always takes care of His people! When your brook dries up, don't panic. The Lord has prepared a means to sustain you. Pay attention. Patiently listen to the voice of the Lord and let Him show you the next step to take. Whether it's at Cherith or at Zarephath, God is going to see to it that you are well taken care of, even in the worst of times.

Maybe you're *Standing At the Edge of the Water.* It might not look like much right now—but it is the water of God's provision.

Perhaps you're at Cherith—the cutting place—and God

has you here with limited resources so that you will learn trust and communion. Maybe your brook has dried up and you need a word of direction from the Lord and a miracle of provision from Him.

His promise is that you are going to be divinely cared for. You're not going under—you are going over. You're not going down to defeat—you are rising up in victory. It doesn't matter how desperate the situation seems, the Lord will come through! When it looks impossible to us—God's just getting started.

CHAPTER 5

THE WATER OF DECISION

I can't remember a time when I wasn't involved in the church. I tell people that I was going to God's house nine months before I was born! My family's heritage in the church traces back to both sets of grandparents.

On my Dad's side, his mother was the first person in her family to turn to Christ. Granddaddy was a sharecropper, barely eking out enough of a living to feed his growing family during the harsh times before and during the Great Depression. An evangelist came to preach a revival in the one-room schoolhouse in the small community and Granny decided to attend one of the services. As she listened to the message of the gospel, the Holy Spirit brought conviction of sin, and that night Granny surrendered her life to Christ.

Such joy filled her heart as she claimed the promise of sins forgiven! But when she returned home and told her husband, he was furious. He blustered, swore, fumed, and finally said, "I forbid you to go back to that meeting. You're not going to bring that religion in here on me and my kids." And then he added, "If you go back down there with *those people* I'll lock you out of the house."

All the next day Granny wrestled with what to do. She wanted to respect her husband and keep the peace in her home, but she also knew she could not deny the transformation that had taken place in her heart. As much as she cared for her family, she valued her relationship with God even more. And so, she made her decision and that evening returned to the revival.

True to his word, when she arrived back home her husband had locked her out of the house. All through the night Granny sat on the porch where she prayed and cried and pleaded with her husband to let her back in. Finally, just before dawn he relented, but once again warned her not to force her new-found religion on him and the kids.

Granny wasn't pushy, but she was persistent. She didn't try to bludgeon him with condemnation and guilt, she just loved him all the more and tried to be the best wife a man could possibly desire. Days turned into weeks...which turned into months...and then years. As he witnessed the transformation that had taken place in the life of his wife and received her unconditional love, finally the heart of my Granddaddy was softened and he, too, responded to the invitation of Christ. Not long after, he suddenly died at a very young age—my father was only five years old at the time.

Granny's decision to obey God, regardless of the cost, became a defining moment in the history of our family. Through her witness, her husband, her mother, and her siblings all came to faith in Christ. From that night of surrendering to the Lord until she finally finished her race at the age of 97, she never once wavered. Our family has been blessed—and through the ministry of five of her children, grandchildren, and great grandchildren who are in full-time vocational ministry, as well as many others of her descendants who faithfully serve the Lord through the ministries of their local church—so have countless others both here and abroad. It is all because of Granny's decision to obey God and trust Him, no matter what.

SAYING NO TO NINEVEH

Most people know Jonah only by the one book of the Bible that bears his name. Not many realize that before the time of this story Jonah was well known as a prophet in Israel. He was considered a God-fearing man—a spiritual leader. The Spirit of the Lord would come upon him and he would speak to the people on behalf of the Lord. He would proclaim, "This is God's Word for your life." He was given insight by the Almighty into events that were going to occur in the future.

At the start of the Book of Jonah, the Lord issues a special call for a ministry task assignment, *"Arise, go to Nineveh the great city and cry against it, for their wickedness has come up before Me"* (Jonah 1:2).

Nineveh was about 500 miles northeast of Jerusalem. It was a major metropolis, but wasn't yet the capital city of Assyria which it would later become. It was known for its beauty, grandeur, and power. The residents of Nineveh were known for their fierceness, their war-like spirit, and also for the atrocities they committed upon whomever they captured.

The Ninevites were the enemies of Israel and Jonah had a big problem with being sent to minister to the very people who would destroy Israel and all its inhabitants if they could. Jonah didn't want to go there. It did not matter that he was a prophet of God or that he was used to hearing the Lord's voice, or that he had been given a definitive directive by the Almighty. In fact, he had a really bad attitude about the whole affair.

Later, in chapter 4, we learn why Jonah was resistant and had such a negative state of mind. His reluctance was because he knew if he went to the Ninevites and they repented, then God would have mercy and spare their lives. Jonah did not want to see this happen. He didn't want to see the Ninevites converted; he wanted that heathen nation destroyed.

Notice the lengths to which Jonah went in order to keep from fulfilling what God wanted him to accomplish. Instead of obeying the Lord's call, packing his bags and heading for Nineveh, Jonah went the opposite direction. He journeyed to Joppa, which was a seaport town. Immediately, he went to the waterfront where he could purchase a ticket on a boat that was sailing *anywhere* except to Nineveh.

So here's Jonah—*Standing At the Edge of the Water*— and it is the water of DECISION. He's waiting his turn in line to buy a ticket. God's call is on his life and the Lord's voice is speaking to him, but there's an internal struggle taking place in his heart. Suddenly it's his turn in line. He steps up to the counter, looks over his options, pays the fare for a passage to Tarshish, receives his ticket, and boards the ship.

This part of the story absolutely shoots the argument of direction by favorable circumstances all to pieces. I've known men and women who have said just like Jonah, "Well it must be okay with God because the circumstances are favorable. After all, I don't want to go to Nineveh, I want to go to Tarshish:

- There's a boat that just happens to be going that direction.
- They just happen to have room for one more passenger.
- I just happen to have enough money for the ticket.
- It's time to board and I just happen to be here just in time."

67

They conclude, "All of the circumstances have worked out so this obviously must be God's will for me."

But consider this:

- Just because there is an open door doesn't always mean God has opened it and wants us to walk through it.
- Just because we are able do something doesn't necessarily mean it's God will for us.
- Just because another job opens up and the salary is greater doesn't automatically mean we should accept the position.

Favorable circumstances represent only one part of the piece of the puzzle of how to discern the will of God. If all we are going on is the fact that the situation looks favorable, we could be making the biggest mistake of our life.

This is exactly what happens to Jonah. The problem was God had specifically stated, "I want you to go to Nineveh." Jonah was in direct defiance of the Almighty, choosing to do something else.

No matter how promising the conditions may appear—if we are in rebellion, God won't bless our endeavors. We can be earning more money than we've ever made in our life, yet be miserable because we won't have the approval of our heavenly Father. And the reason we're missing God's favor is because of our disobedience to His call.

A TICKET TO TURMOIL

God called Jonah to travel 500 miles northeast. Instead he headed 2,000 miles in the opposite direction—all the way to Spain (at least that's where his ticket said he was going). He abandoned his commission and ran from the Lord.

In His rebellion, Jonah took three giant steps *down*:

1. *"He went down to Joppa"* (Jonah 1:3).
2. *"He had gone below [down] into the hold of the ship...and fallen sound asleep"* (verse 5).
3. Finally, they picked up Jonah and *"threw him [down] into the sea"* (verse 15).

Jonah keeps following his own game plan, ignoring what God wants him to do. God calls him—and he runs. The Lord stirs up a storm to stop the smooth sailing of the ship—and Jonah watches as the sailors throw all the cargo overboard. He even has to draw the short straw before finally admitting that he is the reason for the storm.

When it's discovered that Jonah is the cause of the turmoil and the sailors want to know what they should do, instead of falling on his face in repentance before God and suggesting they turn around and return to shore so he can go to Nineveh and fulfill his assignment, Jonah says, *"Pick me up and throw me into the sea. Then the sea will become calm for you"* (verse 12).

Jonah would rather *die* than go to Nineveh. Better to forfeit his life than yield to the will of God.

He was telling those on board, "Throw me over the side of the ship! You'll be saved because I will no longer be with you, and I won't have to go to Nineveh because I'll drown. It will all work out just fine. You'll be okay and so will I."

Seeing no other alternative, the sailors reluctantly tossed him overboard—and the sea grew calm. But instead of drowning, the Lord had prepared a giant fish which swallowed Jonah, and for the next three days and nights, Jonah lay in the belly of that fish. Seaweed wrapped around him. Digestive juices bleached his skin and ate into his flesh. It was dark, smelly, cramped, and uncomfortable. This was nothing like the Disney movie of *Pinocchio*. Gepetto wasn't on a raft with his little fishing pole and a lantern. It was so rough that in chapter 2 Jonah described it as *hell*.

This was as bad as it could get; he was as low as he could go. But there, in the depths of his despair, he finally surrendered to God and began to call out to Him for mercy.

Jonah was at his wit's end, but the Lord heard his cries and gave this giant fish a terrible case of indigestion—and Jonah was vomited up on dry land.

THE THREE "CALLS"

I'm persuaded there may be someone reading this who is in the same kind of desperate situation as Jonah—and the Lord is trying to speak to you. You may not be in the belly of a fish, but you're *Standing At the Edge of the Water*—and it is the water of DECISION.

There isn't a person alive who hasn't been given a call from God. In fact, the Lord issues at least three calls to each and every individual. The answer to the first determines when He gives the second. And the answer to the second determines when He announces the third.

The first call God issues is the call to SALVATION.

You may not even be aware of your need, but if you have never surrendered your life to Jesus Christ and trusted in Him as your only hope of eternal life, the Lord is right now extending to you a call to salvation and asking you to recognize that you are walking away from God and His plan for your life. It is a call to repent of your sin—to acknowledge the death of Jesus Christ on the cross as full payment for the penalty of your sin, to believe in Him as the only begotten Son of God, and to receive Him personally as your Savior by faith.

Every individual has been given this call—to submit; to give up self-control of their life and to put their future in the hands of the Lord Jesus Christ.

If you have never done this, then you are rushing headlong toward eternal destruction. But hear the Lord calling you today. He is offering you abundant life in the present and eternal life in the hereafter. Though you may try to resist...though you may try to run...though you may disregard and rebel against His call—you cannot hide from God.

The second call God issues is a call to SEPARATION.

This divine invitation is to a life that is committed to the Lord in such a fashion that sin is no longer reigning, but you have the victory over it through the power of the Holy Spirit who lives within. It's a call to so submit yourself in obedience to the Holy Spirit that the life of Jesus Christ is lived out through you by His power.

The Lord is asking you to bring every thought you think, every word you speak, every action you take, everything you have, everything you are, the totality of your person, under submission to the Lordship of Jesus Christ. It is a call to become counter-cultural so that you begin to live not so much as a citizen of this world, but as a citizen of a heavenly kingdom.

This is a high and holy calling—to separate from all the manifestations of your former life of sin and begin to live to the praise of His glory and grace. It's a call to holiness, purity, wholeness, and completeness. A call to separation from the old paths unto the new paths, from the old lifestyle unto a new lifestyle—from sin unto righteousness.

The third call God issues is a call to SERVICE.

Whether in the home, the business world, the church, or on the mission field—no matter what or where it is, every person who has responded to the invitation to salvation and separation is then called into service for the Kingdom of God.

The moment you were saved you were signed up to be part of God's army. And your obligation to the Kingdom isn't fulfilled just because you attend church once a week, pay your tithes, give in the offerings, and helped sponsor a missionary. It isn't completed just because you prayed a blessing over your meal, served as an usher, or led a Bible study. God is calling for each of us to draw near to Him—and to keep doing so until, like Moses, we literally glow with His reflected presence. Then we are to take His presence into a lost, darkened world and let the light of His glory shine through us.

He's calling us to actively rescue those who are perishing without a Savior, and to influence our culture for godliness and righteousness.

WHAT WILL IT TAKE?

So many times the Spirit of the Lord deals with our hearts, but we turn Him away. He calls people to repent of their sins and submit their lives to His Lordship—but they keep putting Him off. Over and over He pleads with them to trust Jesus as their only hope of salvation, yet they stubbornly resist. Like Jonah, they insist upon their own independent path. They are determined that if they can just hold out long enough God will eventually see it their way and they can go the direction they always wanted.

It is entirely possible that God is speaking to someone right now. You're *Standing At the Edge of the Water*—and it's the water of DECISION. The questions I have for you are these:

- What will it take to get you to become obedient to the Lord?
- What will it take for you to accept Jesus and repent of your sin?
- What will it take for you to faithfully follow Christ in everything?
- To what extent is God going to have to go in order for you to give up your independence and stop stubbornly shunning His voice?

There's a high price tag on resisting the will of God and hanging onto your stubborn ways. You can't rebel against the Lord without it dearly costing you. And it isn't just YOU that gets hurt—but it puts others close to you in jeopardy as well.

- Parents hurt because their children are refusing the call of God.
- Wives are injured because husbands continue to rebel against the work of the Lord.
- Children are hurting because their parents choose to run from God.

The Holy Spirit is calling. He is trying to get you to release that thing, person, or relationship that has stepped in front of Him and become first priority in your life. God's Spirit is attempting to persuade you to let go of that habit or attitude you stubbornly hang onto which is in opposition to the Father's plan and purpose for your life. He wants you to stop relying on your own ingenuity, strength, and ability, and start trusting in God and God alone.

What will it take before you are willing to surrender to Him? What do you place such high value on that you are willing to forfeit God's best?

A SECOND CHANCE

Some find themselves in the group with Jonah in chapter 1—*Standing At the Edge of the Water* of DECISION. Then there are others who are with Jonah in chapter 3.

In this chapter, Jonah has just been vomited up onto the beach, and he's a mess. Thankfully, that's not the end of the story. The Bible says, *"Now the word of the Lord came to Jonah the second time"* (Jonah 3:1).

In the first instance, once Jonah heard the voice of God, he ran. Now here he is again, standing at the water's edge, and God is giving him another chance to make a *decision*.

This time he gladly runs to Nineveh and begins to proclaim the word of the Lord. Because of his preaching, God brings a revival to the city in which everyone from the White House to the poor house repented and bowed down in worship of Almighty God.

What I want you to understand is that if the Lord would set up circumstance after circumstance in order to get this one rebellious man back onto the right track...if the Lord was willing to speak to His prophet the second time after he went to such great lengths to escape from God's will and plan...then you can be certain He will not give up on you when you blow it.

Most of us recognize the proclivity we have to make mistakes. Sometimes we make them because of ignorance. We make decisions without access to all the data and don't have sufficient information—and we really mess up. Then there are times when, like Jonah, we make mistakes because of willful disobedience, rebellion, and just plain stubbornness. This moves us out of the realm of the mistake and into the place of sin.

The good news is that God doesn't get all bent out of shape when we veer off course. He doesn't intend that our blunders will permanently disable and keep us from productivity. Since the Lord doesn't want sin to be the final word in our life, He will redeem those mistakes—and even those sins—and turn them into lessons that will accomplish His ultimate purpose.

There is a powerful verse in the last book of the Bible, where God declares, *"I am the Alpha and the Omega...who is and who was and who is to come, the Almighty"* (Revelation 1:8).

We know that *Alpha* is the first letter of the Greek alphabet. It's the starting point. And in this verse, God says that He is the beginning—the *Alpha.*

- It's not just that in the beginning God created the heavens and the earth.
- It's not just that God was the beginning of a fresh, new world after the flood.
- It's not just that God was the beginning of a new nation from the seed of Abraham.
- It's not just that God was the beginning of a messianic dynasty that began with a covenant with David.
- It's not just that He was the beginning of a new covenant at the birth, death, and resurrection of Jesus Christ.

75

- It's not just that He was the beginning of a new age with the coming of the Holy Spirit and the establishment of the church.
- It's not just that He was the beginning of a new life when we were born again by the Spirit.

God is *still* the Beginner. He is *still Alpha*. He is *still* the Almighty God of new beginnings. Right now—this very minute—to you personally—He is *Alpha*. He did not say, "I was Alpha and I will be Omega." Nor did He declare, "I used to be Alpha." Instead, He proclaims, "I AM...I AM a fresh beginning." He is in a constant state of beginning and a continual state of completion.

This means that no matter how horribly we fail—when we make a mistake, turn down the wrong path, look to the wrong sources, listen to conflicting voices, give in to the temptation and the pressure around us, or even willfully rebel and make decisions in direct violation of God's will and purpose—*at that moment*, He is mighty to bring a fresh beginning to our life. At that exact time, He is the ever-present *Alpha* who says, "It's time for a new beginning." In an instant, He is the One who promises, "Behold, I make all things new."

We have seen Him as the baby lying in a manger, as the Son of God walking on the shores of Galilee, as the man of sorrows acquainted with grief, and as the Savior lifted up on the cross. Now it's time we saw Him as the Almighty —powerful enough to turn all our mistakes, our wrong choices, even our most wicked of sins, into a fresh start which He will bring to completion to the praise of His glory.

FOUR STEPS TO YOUR TURN-AROUND

Perhaps you are with Jonah—*Standing At the Edge of the Water.* You've heard a word of hope as you've been reading this story, but your life is in shambles. You've made terrible mistakes, ignored God, and gone your own way. Now you're wanting to know how it can be totally changed. Let me quickly give you four steps that can help turn it all around.

Step number 1: BEGIN WHERE YOU ARE

I meet so many who are waiting to read just one more book, or attend one more seminar, or get to one more counselor, or learn just one more piece of information—and then they'll get started in a new direction.

What you need to know is that you can't correct the problems in your life by yourself. When you have been disobedient or have made wrong decisions, you may try moving to another location, launching another business, entering another relationship, and starting a new life; but unless you have placed God as the center, it won't be long before the new plan is as messed up as the old one was.

In chapter 2 of Jonah, we find, *"Then Jonah prayed to the Lord his God from the stomach of the fish, and he said, 'I called out of my distress to the Lord, and He answered me'"* (verses 1-2).

Jonah couldn't wait until the mistakes he had made had been corrected and his feet were firmly back on dry land. Every time he tried to fix his errors, he only made them worse. So Jonah started right where he was—in the stomach of the fish, in the midst of his suffering. That seems like a most unlikely place for a prayer meeting, but this was desperation time. Jonah began right there, calling on the Lord for a fresh start.

77

Today, where you are at this very moment, is the best place to begin, with God's help, turning this whole thing around—making right choices, godly decisions, and being obedient to the will, the voice, and the plan of God which He speaks to you.

Step number 2: REPENT

You may have gone your own way, left God out of your life, and made poor decisions—whether out of stubbornness and rebellion or simply out of ignorance. It's time for a turn-around. The repentant heart is always a proper posture toward God. This is why David sang in Psalm 51:17, *"The sacrifices of God are a broken spirit; a broken and a contrite heart, O God, You will not despise."*

In the middle of Jonah's greatest distress he cried out to the Lord in repentance, "God, I blew it! God, I messed up! I'm sorry. Please forgive me."

Here's the marvelous promise of the Almighty to all who are contrite: *"I have wiped out your transgressions like a thick cloud and your sins like a heavy mist. Return to Me, for I have redeemed you"* (Isaiah 44:22).

Remember this guarantee: *"The Lord is near to those who have a broken heart and saves such as have a contrite spirit"* (Psalm 34:18 NKJV).

The biggest mistake you can ever make is to leave God out of the picture. But when you want to leave the past behind, repent—put God back in the middle where He belongs. He promises to abundantly pardon your past.

Step number three: FORGIVE YOURSELF

I have seen people who were crippled spiritually, emotionally, and psychologically, stunted in their growth and paralyzed with fear because they have never forgiven themselves. Every time they start to do something significant for the Lord, the enemy of their soul throws up a mental image of their last mistake. They keep dwelling on the past and focusing on the negatives.

It's time to stop listening to the accusations, condemnations, and lies of the devil and tune your ear to the Word of God which says , *"You will know the truth, and the truth shall make you free"*(John 8:32). Start believing, *"If the Son makes you free, you shall be free indeed"* (verse 36 NKJV).

Claim the promise of God that you are redeemed. You are released from the prison of your mistakes; no longer bound by the errors of the past. Now you are forgiven in the name of the Lord Jesus Christ, and are more than a conqueror through His power that is at work in your life.

Step number four: DARE TO TRY AGAIN

There are a number of lessons we learn from the narrative of Jonah, but one of the most important verses to me in the entire story is one I mentioned earlier: *"Now the word of the Lord came to Jonah the second time"* (Jonah 3:1).

I don't know anybody who was successful in making it across the room the first time they tried to walk. When a baby is taking its first steps and his legs crumble beneath him, we don't grab the toddler and cry, "Oh, bless his heart. He fell. We'll just carry him from now until Jesus comes!"

Instead, we rush over to the baby, give him a cuddle and say, "Here, let Mama kiss the boo-boo." Daddy will chime in, "Come on, big guy, get up. You can do it. Come on, buddy, come to Daddy!"

We catch, steady, and encourage the child. We get him back on his feet again as quickly as possible.

No matter how many times you've started with the Lord

and then stopped...or tried and then failed...it's time to get up, brush yourself off, let the Lord Jesus kiss away the hurt, and dare to try again. The only thing that will constitute failure is if you remain down and refuse to get back up.

Mistakes do not disqualify you for use in the Kingdom. Thankfully, our God is the God of the second chance. So you blew it; so you failed; so you sinned. Perhaps you even rebelled against the Lord, ignoring Him, rejecting His plan. God is saying to you, "Get up! Resist fear! Make Me your partner! Dare to try again!"

THE CHOICE IS YOURS

Jonah is thrown up onto the beach out of the belly of the fish. Once more he's at a place of *decision*. Does he go home humiliated, ignoring the voice of God again? Does he keep kicking himself because of his boneheaded decisions the first time? Or does he make God his partner, beginning where he is, repenting of past mistakes, forgiving himself, and daring to try once more?

Jonah chose the path of surrender and obedience. He looked up to heaven and said, "I'll try again!" And Nineveh turned to the Lord at the preaching of the prophet of God.

If you're *Standing At the Edge of the Water* of DECISION, wondering if the Lord could really be speaking to you, doubting whether God can really use you—dare to try again. Then watch what the Lord does with someone who will be obedient to Him.

CHAPTER 6

THE WATER OF LIFE

Ezekiel was one of the young men carried into exile by the Babylonians when they conquered Jerusalem around 586 BC. He was part of the priestly family and was himself a priest. But while he was living in captivity he was also called by God to be a prophet, and it is from this role that we have the book that bears his name.

During the time when Ezekiel and the people of God were in exile, the Lord began giving him visions of things that were to come—including what lay ahead for the land of Israel and specifically the city of Jerusalem.

Some of the visions given to him speak of God's judgment and punishment upon His people because of their sin and wickedness. In addition, there is a series of prophecies concerning other nations of the world that were in existence during this time, and they are words of judgment, rebuke, and lamentation because of the evil that was being committed by them.

As we read these prophetic words, we discover that what was spoken against those nations is rather bleak. At the same time, Ezekiel's ministry was not completely negative, because right on the heels of some of his gravest warnings, the Lord gave him a series of visions that were full of hope and encouragement for the people of God.

The word of the Lord through the prophet Ezekiel revealed that there was going to come a day when God would once again visit His people, restore their fortunes, and set up His kingdom in their midst—a kingdom of righteousness and peace.

"IN THE MIDST"

There is a Hebrew word that keeps cropping up in the writings of Ezekiel that helps us see just how he saw his role and his relationship with those to whom he was to minister. The word that is used is translated for us as *among* or *in the midst*—and it is used 116 times in this book; more than in any other Old Testament book. Ezekiel's consciousness of his place *in the midst* of crisis and *in the midst* of a ministry to people was unique to the prophets of the Old Testament.

Back in Jerusalem, Ezekiel had lived *in the midst* of a world renown religious, trade, and travel center. He was taken captive and placed *in the midst* of Babylon, another noted world empire where he was called to be a spokesman for God to an unreceiving and unwelcoming audience. Near the end of his ministry he was transported through visions *in the midst* of a coming ideal kingdom. The final revelation that is recorded at the conclusion of the book positioned Ezekiel *in the midst* of an end-time city called "Jehovah-Shammah"—"The Lord is There."

What Ezekiel discovered is the same thing you and I need to remember today. We must learn that:

- *In the midst* of all the changes of life—the Lord reigns supreme.
- *In the midst* of the storms—God is on His throne.
- *In the midst* of a sinful world—the Almighty remains holy and righteous.

82

- *In the midst* of a world of nations who set themselves against God—He is a reprover and refiner.
- *In the midst* of shattered dreams—He is the God who redeems and restores.
- *In the midst* of a world of strife—He is the hope of a coming reign of peace.
- *In the midst* of a world of sin and death—He is our hope of eternal life.

Praise God! He is still *in the midst* of His people.

When our world seems torn and shaken and completely broken apart; just when it looks like it's been abandoned by everything good, decent, and right, if we'll look around us a little more carefully we will find that God is right there *in the midst* of it all. He hasn't abandoned this world to chance and happenstance. He hasn't relinquished His scepter of authority to another, nor has He gone on a far journey and left us to our own devices. He is still sitting with the heavens as His throne and the earth as His footstool.

God remains in control. This is my Father's world and He is still orchestrating all the diverse pieces; bringing them together in a grand symphony which is one day going to come to a majestic climax that will rise to the praise of His glory. The final outcome toward which all this is moving is that the kingdoms of this world will become the Kingdom of our Lord and of His Christ, and He shall reign forever and forever. And of His Kingdom there shall be no end. Every knee shall bow, and every tongue shall confess that Jesus Christ is Lord to the glory of God the Father!

VISIONS OF RESTORATION

Now we find Ezekiel *in the midst* of exile and bondage, and the Lord begins to give him visions of restoration. They are words of encouragement and comfort in the midst of captivity.

Starting in Ezekiel 40 we have the record of a series of visions which were revealed to him concerning the restoration of the Temple in Jerusalem, the renewal of the priesthood, and the boundaries of the land which are going to make up the restored Kingdom.

When the Babylonians came to conquer Jerusalem and exile the people of God, the Temple was completely destroyed. The gold plating was stripped from the inside walls. The vessels dedicated for use in worship were boxed up and carried away.

The gates of the city were the symbols and representation of authority and power. As long as the gates were intact you could defend against intruders, but the gates had been broken down and burned, so Jerusalem and all its inhabitants were completely vulnerable.

Yet *in the midst* of Ezekiel's exile God starts giving him visions of the restoration of the Temple and of the city. He begins speaking to him, saying, "I know what it was like when you left. As you began your journey toward Babylon you looked back over your shoulder and saw the smoke rising from the ruins. But I want you to know, Ezekiel, another day is on the horizon. Not only am I going to rebuild that holy place, but I'm also going to restore those who minister there—I am bringing back the priesthood. There is going to be a holy remnant that will come back together. Once again there will be a high priest in My Temple, and sacrifices of praise will be offered up to Me."

The visions are quite detailed, and like most prophetic words, they speak to us on more than one level. These are revelations in which God is pulling back the curtain on the coming physical restoration He will bring about in the last days. They are literal descriptions of what God is yet going to do in the land of Israel, and they correspond in scope and detail to the picture we are given in the Book of the Revelation regarding what will take place at the end of this age.

But while there is yet to come a literal fulfillment of these visions, they don't just speak of a physical reality, but on a spiritual level as well—applying to where we are living today, which brings us to what is written in chapter 47.

FRESH, HEALING WATER

According to the vision given to Ezekiel, when the nation of Israel is fully restored, when the Temple is rebuilt and the priesthood is reestablished, there is going to be a river of water that is going to flow out from underneath the threshold of the Temple on the eastern side. This river will run from the Temple all the way to the Dead Sea. It's going to be fresh, healing water that will bring life to a parched, desert land. It will be so full of vitality that even the Dead Sea will be teeming with new life when this river begins to flow into it.

In the vision of chapter 47, the angelic messenger is taking Ezekiel all around the rebuilt Temple. They are measuring the rooms and taking the dimensions of the outside walls and noting the placement of all the gates. Then this messenger from God brings Ezekiel back around to the front of the Temple which faces east and shows him the water that is flowing out from under the threshold.

The first thing that is unusual about this river of water is that it begins as just a trickle, but it quickly increases in breadth and depth. The longer it runs, the larger it becomes. And here's Ezekiel, *Standing At the Edge of the Water*—and it is the water of LIFE. And the angel says to him, "Come with me. Come into the water."

As they walk into the water they carry a measuring line. They measure a thousand cubits—and the water is ankle-deep. They continue into the river another thousand cubits —and the water is to the knees. Yet another thousand cubits is measured—and the water rises to their loins. The measurement of one more thousand cubits is recorded—and the water is too deep to touch bottom; it's a river that can't be forded; you have to swim across.

This water is more than something that is going to be a physical reality during the coming earthly Kingdom of our Lord; more than just a prophetic vision of what is going to happen in the end times. This also has significance for where we find ourselves today.

When Jesus walked this earth, He told the woman at the well about water that would come from Him. He said, *"Everyone who drinks of this water will thirst again; but whoever drinks of the water that I will give him shall never thirst; but the water that I will give him will become in him a well of water springing up to eternal life"* (John 4:13-14).

Later, we find Jesus standing up on the last day of the Feast of Tabernacles, crying out, *"If any man is thirsty, let him come to Me and drink. He who believes in Me, as the Scripture said, 'From his innermost being shall flow rivers of living water'"* (John 7:37-38).

The next verse explains what the Son of God was referring to: *"But this He spoke of the Spirit, whom those who believed in Him were to receive"* (verse 39).

A NEVER-ENDING RIVER

Reading about this water in Ezekiel reminds me of the psalmist singing, *"How blessed is the man who does not walk in the counsel of the wicked, nor stand in the path of sinners, nor sit in the seat of scoffers! But his delight is in the law of the Lord, and in His law he meditates day and night. He will be like a tree firmly planted by streams of water, which yields its fruit in its season, and its leaf does not wither; and in whatever he does, he prospers"* (Psalm 1:1-3).

The water that Ezekiel is shown started all the way back with the river that was flowing in the very beginning in the Garden, and it winds through Scripture until the very end in the Book of the Revelation. It's the water of the Spirit.

It begins as a well of salvation, then it runs like a mighty river of the Spirit. It is water that we are going to be able to be firmly planted beside—and sink our roots deep into. And from that spiritual nourishment life is going to spring forth.

The physical water in Ezekiel 47 is not only real water that will flow during the earthly Kingdom rule and reign of our Lord, but it is also a representation of a spiritual truth. Just as the physical water brings healing and life to the parched earth and Dead Sea, even so there is spiritual water that is "living," and it flows to the heart and life of one who is dead in trespasses and sins, bringing healing to the soul, and springing up to eternal life.

Is your walk lifeless, empty, and nonproductive? Are you just going through the motions, and struggling without anything to show for your efforts? If so, the Lord has brought you to the place where He has you *Standing At the Edge of the Water*—and it's the water of LIFE.

Even now, He is saying, "Take My hand...and let's step into the water."

There is a river of the Spirit of God that is spreading all over this earth, bringing renewal and revival in places where we once thought it was impossible to reach. The Lord is doing a work of the Spirit today in the hearts and lives of those who thirst for the things of God. He is speaking to every man, woman, and young person who will give attention to His words. He is imploring, "Come into the river; into the flow of what I'm doing in this day. Get into the place of My Spirit because there is a work I want you to experience as a present reality in your own life. So step into the river!"

WHY SIT ON THE BANKS?

The truth is that there are people who hear this message and see what God is doing, but instead of stepping into the river and experiencing the fresh stream of God's Spirit, they simply sit on the bank and watch what happens when others wade into the waters.

God is inviting them: "Come on in. Get into the river." But many say, "No thank You. I'm happy to just sit here and watch."

Some are relaxing on the bank of the river, and they are being *entertained.* It's fun to see what happens when a person really begins to experience the fresh flow of God's Spirit. They like to be in the atmosphere where the Spirit is present, but they're not completely sure they actually want to become involved themselves. Some even cross the line of entertainment into mockery and ridicule—they begin to poke fun at what God is doing and how people respond when God's Spirit touches them.

There are others who sit on the bank of the river of the Spirit of God and *criticize* those who are immersed in the river. When God's Spirit begins to move in a certain way, they find fault because they've never seen Him work like that before.

They see somebody swimming in the blessings of the Almighty and all they want to do is belittle the technique and sneer at the method. They criticize the stroke (why are they doing the backstroke when they should be doing the breaststroke?).

People have all kinds of reactions when the Spirit of God begins to flow in their lives. Some laugh; others cry; some shout; others fall down; some dance; others sing; some do all of the above.

When the Spirit begins to move, it sometimes means the service order gets turned around or programs are cancelled. Perhaps the things we expect to happen, don't—and the things we never dreamed would happen, do.

One thing is for sure. You can't stay the same way you've always been when the current of God's Spirit begins to move to you and through you. When you step into the heavenly river of anointing it will change you, challenge you, and motivate you in ways you never thought possible.

There are those who want things to be different without anything changing. They don't want to leave their comfort zone. They don't want anything they can't control or are unable to predict. So they would rather sit on the bank of the river and criticize.

The Lord calls us into the river, but there are too many who would rather laze on the bank and never venture in...until some kind of trouble or crisis arises. Then all they want is to just dip their feet in and wade around in ankle-deep water.

They may want to be touched and refreshed by the Spirit, but not to be changed by His power. They certainly don't want to be carried along to the place where they can't touch bottom.

However, the deep water is where the Lord longs to bring us. He wants to lead us past the point of refreshing at the ankles, and past the depth of the knees where we can cleanse ourselves. God even wants to lead us beyond the depth of the loins which is the place of power. He desires to bring us all the way into the river until we can't touch bottom—and we are swept along by the current of His divine Spirit; where all we can do is simply trust that He's going to bring us to the place in Him that is best for our lives.

God is longing to bring us into the deep where we confess, "I can't trust my own strength. I can't depend on being able to touch bottom. I can't rely on what I've always known to be true. Lord, I've got to trust You."

A RIVER OF LIFE!

Here is one of the most exciting details of Ezekiel's prophetic vision: *"It will come about that every living creature which swarms in every place where the river goes, will live. And there will be very many fish, for these waters go there and the others become fresh; so everything will live where the river goes"* (Ezekiel 47:9).

Remember, the prophet is in exile, prophesying to those in captivity. The memory of the destruction of their Temple is still very real to them. The remembrance of their slain loved ones lying on the ground remains a very vivid, painful picture.

Not only that, but when Ezekiel began to speak about the Dead Sea, the people would immediately know what he was talking about. It isn't called the *Dead* Sea for nothing. It has no life. Normal sea water contains anywhere from four to six percent minerals, but the Dead Sea has 24 to 26 percent minerals. People don't fish in its waters, at least not those who expect to catch anything. It's stagnant; it's dead!

But hear what the Lord has to say. To those who are exiled from their homeland and held in the bondage of captivity, to the Israelites who readily identify with the lifelessness of the Dead Sea, God speaks through the prophet and proclaims: "I've got a river. It is one of life. And there's

90

going to come a time when this river is going to flow from underneath the threshold of My holy Temple. And everywhere this river runs it will bring life. It will flow through the desert, and cause it to blossom like a rose. It will wind through the wasteland, where trees will sprout on both banks...and those trees are going to bear fruit in their season...and the leaves of those trees are going to be leaves of healing."

The Lord adds, "This river is going to continue until it reaches the Dead Sea. And the thing that looks like it will never be productive or sustain any life is going to become alive and teeming with fish. Because everywhere My river flows and everything the water of My river touches is going to spring forth with new life!"

REFRESHING WATER

I believe the Lord is speaking to an individual right now who has ears to hear:

- He is speaking to someone whose dreams have been broken on the rocks of harsh reality.
- He is speaking to someone whose hopes have been dashed and ruined.
- He is speaking to someone who has worked hard but has nothing to show for the effort.
- He is speaking to someone whose spiritual life has become dry and barren.
- He is speaking to someone who has been through one failed relationship after another.
- He is speaking to someone who's tried everything they know, but can't seem to find satisfaction or fulfillment.

- He is speaking to someone whose failures have brought them to the depths of despair.
- He is speaking to someone who has become so desperate that they have decided life isn't worth living.

The Lord is saying: "I've got a river—a river of LIFE. It is flowing, and everything its water touches gains new hope, new health, new life. Everywhere it flows there is refreshing...there is fruitfulness."

So if you're tired of hurting, struggling, and weary with the way things are; if you are fed up with everything falling apart and feel like something within you has withered and died, then step into the river of God's Spirit that's flowing to you right now.

When you do, the Lord is going to bring you *life.* You'll not be depressed or discouraged. He will cause you to once again be fruitful. The very place where you thought you were dead and would be productive no more—that's where this exciting *new, refreshing life* is going to spring forth.

It doesn't matter how long it's been dead within you, the Lord says LIVE!

Not only are you going to blossom, but you will also be an agent of God's healing grace to reach out to others who are despairing and in captivity.

- God is calling for marriage partners to step into the river together.
- God is calling for business owners to step into the river.
- God is calling for those who have become discouraged in ministry to step into the river.
- God is calling for individuals who have been wounded by a friend to step into the river.

- God is calling for someone who has suffered because of a false accusation to step into the river.
- God is calling for the person who has grown cold and passive in their walk with the Lord to step into the river.
- God is calling for everyone who needs to be renewed and refreshed in their spirit to step into the river.

By faith, take that first step—because everywhere the river flows, there is LIFE.

CHAPTER 7

THE WATER OF POWERFUL ANOINTING

W e live in desperate times. The late Vance Havner defined the problem of this age by saying, "There is *anarchy* in the world...there is *apostasy* in the church...and there is *apathy* in the pew."

One of the major problems we have in the modern church is that too many of our constituents are living spiritually anemic lives. We're centered on self rather than on the purposes of God—more interested in how we feel and what we are going to attain in the present than we are in the eternal goals of the Kingdom.

Our needs are no different from believers who have lived before us:

- To be *filled* with the Spirit.
- To *walk* in the Spirit.
- To *live* in the Spirit.
- To be *immersed* in the Spirit.
- To be *baptized* in the Spirit.
- To be *overwhelmed* by the Spirit.

It is imperative for men and women who are born again to be powerfully *anointed* by God's Spirit so that every chain is broken, every bondage is loosed, and every captive is freed. It's the anointing that will make the difference on our planet; that will cause an unrighteous world to sit up and take notice and enable us to achieve what the Lord has called and commissioned us to do.

We are in dire need of the anointing of the Spirit of God!

There was an Old Testament prophet who understood this only too well. His name was Elisha—a protégé of Elijah (2 Kings 2:1-15). He hadn't campaigned for the job. In fact, when he was called by Elijah he was at the tail end of a group of workers who were plowing a field with yokes of oxen and they were kicking up dust in his face. He wasn't looking for a "prophet" position; he was just trying to keep his nose out of the dirt so that he could breathe.

But Elijah came by one day, under the leading of the Spirit of God, and cast his mantle over the shoulders of Elisha, and the farmer was called into ministry.

Elisha was Elijah's helper and co-worker, a prophet in training. He had seen God's hand of powerful anointing upon Elijah as this great prophet had boldly declared the word of the Lord, sometimes under the worst of conditions.

As he walked and worked with Elijah, observing the Spirit of the Lord upon the prophet's life, something stirred within the heart of Elisha. He recognized a powerful anointing of God and he knew that if he was going to fulfill the call of the Almighty, he was going to need this same kind of anointing.

In this story we have a prophet who sees a dimension of God's grace and power that he does not yet possess. And the account illustrates for us the kind of process that is involved in receiving powerful anointing.

SEPARATION FROM THE WORLD

The journey of these two men begins at a location called *Gilgal.* This was the first place Israel came after crossing the

Jordan into the promised land of Canaan. It was at Gilgal they stopped and circumcised all the males who had been born during the time of wandering in the wilderness because they had not received the mark of the covenant of God—meaning they were not full participants and partakers of the Lord's covenant blessing.

Gilgal means *"the reproach is rolled away."* It was here —through the rite of circumcision in which the children of Israel once more identified themselves as the covenant people of God—that the shame of Egypt was rolled away. Gilgal speaks to us about the place of being separated from the world, and where the identification with what is in opposition to the things of God is removed from our lives.

If we long to experience powerful anointing, it begins by being set apart from the world. It starts with entering into a covenant relationship with the heavenly Father through faith in Jesus Christ, His only begotten Son.

The "beginning place" for the anointing that will release us from the bondage of destruction is to kneel at an altar of prayer, repent of our sins, and surrender the control of our life to Christ. We come, just as we are, to God through faith in Jesus. And because of faith in the sacrifice of Christ as the only acceptable payment for sin, we are declared righteous. Old things pass away; all things become new. None of this happens because we earned or deserved it, but just because God loves us and extends His grace, which is absolutely amazing.

Gilgal is where we are separated from sin unto God —where we recognize our need for a Savior and fall upon the mercy of God. Then He meets with us and imparts His divine nature of holiness and declares us holy, because when He touches us, we become like Him.

The process starts at Gilgal where Elijah said to Elisha, "Why don't you just stay here?" But Elisha responded,

"Absolutely not. I've seen something else. Salvation is wonderful. I appreciate having my sins forgiven. I am grateful for being touched by the presence of God. I like having the reproach of sin taken away so that I don't bear the guilt and shame of my past any more. I am blessed being marked with the holiness of God. I like being identified as a partaker of God's covenant of blessing. But I've seen something else. I have a desire for more of God. I want to walk in a greater dynamic of His grace and power than just being seen as part of the family. I'm not staying here when there is the possibility of something greater. I am going with YOU. Wherever you go, I'm going."

The reality is this: assurance of sins forgiven is a powerful truth. Being cleansed from iniquity is an incredible experience, but the promise of God is that there is so much more. The call from heaven is always higher, broader, greater, and deeper.

If we want to receive the powerful anointing that is so needed and is promised by God we have to travel a path He has planned. And the next stop in the journey takes us to *Bethel.*

BETHEL—THE HOUSE OF GOD

In Genesis 28 we find the account of Jacob spending the night at a certain spot and using a stone for a pillow. In the middle of the night he had a dream about a ladder set on the earth with its top reaching into heaven. There were angels ascending and descending on that ladder. And the Lord spoke to him in the dream—words of promise and blessing. It was the same blessing that had been spoken to Abraham many years before.

The Bible tells us that Jacob awoke from his sleep and said, *"Surely the Lord is in this place, and I did not know it"*

97

(verse 16). Then we see that he was fearful and afraid, adding, *"How awesome is this place! This is none other than the house of God and this is the gate of heaven"* (verse 17).

Jacob named where he was, *Bethel*, which means *house of God*. He took the stone that had served as a pillow and set it up as an altar. Then he poured oil over it and prayed and made a vow to God on that very spot.

Bethel is the house of the Lord, the place of prayer and worship where God meets with man and man meets with God. It's the site of divine promise and blessing.

Years after this initial encounter with God at Bethel the Lord spoke to Jacob again. He gathered up all his household and said, "We're going *back* to Bethel." They separated themselves from the false idols that were among them. They recommitted themselves to serving the Lord and returned to this place of blessing—back to an altar of divine promise.

When they reached Bethel, Jacob had a fresh encounter with the Lord. He renamed the place *El-Bethel*. In earlier days it had been called simply *Bethel*—the house of God. Now he calls it *El-Bethel*—God of the house of God.

What Jacob discovered is that the really important thing is not the location. As wonderful and defining as the landmark was in his life, he realized that it wasn't nearly as significant to revisit the house of God as it was to spend personal time with the God of the house.

BEYOND A "TOUCH"

In receiving the promised powerful anointing it is essential to recognize that no sooner do we come from Gilgal, where sins are forgiven and the guilt, shame, and reproach are rolled away, than God wants to get us to His house—the place of worship and prayer, where He can meet with us and bring promise and favor to our life.

God has tremendous blessings He wants to pour out on those who gather in His house. He makes incredible promises to those who separate from the things of the world and unite together in His sanctuary.

There are marvelous spiritual experiences that can only happen to us when we meet with Him in His house. It's there that we will have divine encounters with the God of the house and our life will never be the same.

But please understand this: the Lord's blessings and promises of help are not the powerful anointing. The touch of God isn't the same as being anointed by God.

Throughout the Bible when people are *touched* by the Lord, they are often overwhelmed by His power—and they fall down before Him. But when individuals are *anointed* by God they are made to stand up on their feet and sent out to do the work of the Lord.

Too many are praying for the touch of God, when instead He is wanting to anoint us—to empower and enable us.

This is what we see happening in the life of another prophet, Isaiah. Read how he describes his awesome awareness of God: *"I saw the Lord sitting on a throne, lofty and exalted, with the train of His robe filling the temple"* (Isaiah 6:1).

The cherubim are on either side of the throne and they're crying, *"Holy, Holy, Holy!"* The doors are shaking at the sound of those who are crying out.

Scripture tells us that he fell on his face. Isaiah has just had an incredible encounter with the power and majesty of God and he couldn't stand upright any longer.

Then the Lord sends one of those angels to the altar with tongs. He takes a coal from the altar and touches the lips of the prophet; in essence, anointing him.

Next, God asks, *" Who can I send? Who will go for Me?"* And Isaiah stands up and answers, *"Here am I. Send me."*

He couldn't say those words when he had only been touched by God or had a personal meeting with the Lord; not even when he had the revelation of the Father's glory. But when he was *anointed* by God, then he could boldly march forward and do something extraordinary for the Kingdom.

ON TO JERICHO

There are some who are content to remain at Bethel. Their sins are forgiven, they attend a wonderful church, worship, and enjoy a good life. What could be better?

Elijah tried to encourage Elisha to remain at Bethel. In fact, the sons of the prophets who were there tried to get Elisha to stay with them. They were telling him, "Look at the blessings and the glorious worship. See the promises of God we're receiving. We have a powerful, growing, successful church. Why not stay and be content right here?"

But Elisha had caught a glimpse of something more; something far greater. Over and over he said to Elijah, "*As the Lord lives, and as you yourself live, I will not leave you.*"

So together, they traveled to *Jericho.*

Jericho was the first city Israel conquered after crossing into the promised land. It was the "first-fruits" victory, and in the economy of God, the first fruits always belong to the Lord. They are set apart and considered holy to Him.

Gilgal speaks of being separated unto God. Bethel speaks of loosening the ties to the things of the world. Jericho speaks of our possessions being committed unto God.

When we read about the conquering of Jericho there is another story that is told alongside the main event—the account of Achan (Joshua 7).

The Lord instructed the people of Israel not to take any of the bounty of Jericho for themselves. Silver, gold, precious gems—anything of value was to be brought to the Lord. All of the goods of the city were considered "accursed" to the Israelites because they were to be set aside to be given for God's work.

Achan plundered some of the valuables of Jericho and hid them in the dirt under his tent. Because of his sin, 36 soldiers lost their lives and Israel was defeated in the battle against the small town of Ai.

There is much to learn from the story of Achan. Maybe you feel like you're a person of little or no consequence in the congregation. You are minding your own business, except you have this one small thing you like to do on the side, thinking no one is watching. However, if your actions are not in keeping with the will of God and His purpose, the Lord calls it sin. Even though you're just one insignificant individual in the midst of several hundred, one person can cause an entire congregation to lose their spiritual vitality.

The New Testament makes a point of telling us that we are the body of Christ. What I do affects you and what you do affects me. One member of the body can have an impact on the entire body. When we decide we're going to do *what* we want, *when* we want, and *how* we want, we are not just affecting ourselves, but the whole congregation.

At Gilgal we make a commitment of our lives to God. At Bethel we separate ourselves from the world unto the purposes of God. But at Jericho we go even further and commit all the *things* of our lives. Not only must we be dedicated to the Lord, but every area and everything must be committed to Him.

So many times we want God's power and blessings, but we have a hard time surrendering the "stuff." It's the idea of being completely sold out and dedicated to the Lord. At Jericho we surrender all we have, all we are, and all we hope to be.

It is here that we offer Him our relationships, jobs, talents, possessions, and recreation...everything—totally and completely. We say, "Nothing I am and nothing I have is more important than You and Your anointing."

Jericho is the place where *things* are separated unto God. The only way we can then touch a particular item again is if the Lord puts it back into our hands to use as good stewards until He calls for it. And when we use it, we do so only to the praise of His glory.

Every time I read this story I am struck by the tenacity of Elisha. He was not going to be put off or denied; he was determined to have this anointing.

RECEIVE THE MANTLE

One of the greatest temptations we will experience in our spiritual walk is that of becoming complacent. At each level of new growth, we are tempted to remain where we are and be content. Some of us reach the place where God's Spirit is at work—the blessings are flowing and the promises are coming—and we begin to think that just because God promised something then all we have to do is sit down and await its arrival.

This is not the lesson from Elisha. Even though a blessing is available from God and promised by Him, we must pursue it. We can't work hard to somehow *earn* the anointing, but it's also true that we won't receive this power if we don't diligently and faithfully seek what the Lord offers.

I can't speak for you. But as for me, I want all of God that I can possibly get. Somehow I have a feeling that there is a more dynamic dimension of God's power and anointing than anything I've ever been privileged to experience. And I'm not going to be satisfied until I know the fullness of all He has for me.

I want a powerful anointing—one that will break chains of

bondage, tear down strongholds in the kingdom of darkness, and be a life-changing force in the Kingdom of God.

Elisha stands his ground and will not give up. He crosses the Jordan with Elijah and makes his request for a double portion. He keeps his eyes open. The chariots and horsemen of fire come and the whirlwind catches them and the prophet away—and Elisha sees it all. He watches as they disappear into the sky.

Then he reaches down and picks up the mantle of Elijah. Most translations are somewhat misleading when they say the mantle "fell" from Elijah. That word really means it was "thrown down with a purpose."

Elisha was faithful, diligent, watchful, and would not be denied. He was willing to go through whatever it took to receive the promise, and his reward was the mantle of Elijah.

See him as he makes his journey back to the Jordan River, mantle in hand, *Standing At the Edge of the Water.*

Elisha has been a good pupil. He carefully observed Elijah. He rolls up the mantle and calls out, *"Where is the Lord, God of Elijah?"* (2 Kings 2:14).

He must have thought, "I have the mantle, but do I also have the anointing that goes with it?"

Then he strikes the water, and it parts! At that moment, the sons of the prophets recognize, "The spirit of Elijah rests on Elisha!" (verse 15).

The truth is, those around you will know when the Spirit of God is resting on your life. You won't have to wear a big button that reads, "I'm anointed." They will know because you will walk into your job Monday morning and exude a confidence you never had before. When you encounter obstacles there will be a cool calmness about you and an ability to make correct decisions quickly. You won't have to advertise, but others will recognize that something is definitely different.

The sons of the prophets exclaimed, "I see it." They saw the manifestation that the Spirit which had been on Elijah was now on Elisha.

That same powerful anointing can be ours as well—if we are willing to go through God's process, refusing to give up.

The problem in the church today is that many are seeking the *things* of the Spirit, but precious few are truly seeking the Spirit Himself. They desire the promises, the blessings, and the manifestations, but where are those who want Him—His presence, His glory, and His anointing? Many seek His hand—but not His face.

THE PROCESS THAT LEADS TO POWER

Years later we find Elisha preparing to die, and he is visited by Joash, the king of Israel (2 Kings 13). He tells Joash to take arrows and strike the ground and shoot them out the window, and the actions have a prophetic significance.

This king wasn't a righteous leader, but while Elisha is drawing his final breath Joash cries out, *"My father, my father, the chariots of Israel and its horsemen!"* (verse 14). These were the same words spoken by Elisha at the catching away of Elijah (2 Kings 2:12).

The king knows the story; he remembers the formula, but he doesn't have the power. He is saying all the right words, yet lacks the anointing. He hasn't been to Gilgal, Bethel, or Jericho. Instead of going through the process, he tried a short cut.

Even now, we have men and women saying, "In Jesus' name," wanting to produce miracles and cast out demons. They have a *form* of godliness, but are void of the *power* of godliness. That kind of power and anointing only comes when you follow the steps given by God.

Today the Lord wants to put within your heart a desire for

something more—a holy discontent with the status quo. He is anxious to give you a longing for something greater. This anointing isn't just for pastors, missionaries, or church leaders, but it's for you—right where you live. It is yours if you'll follow God's plan.

Right now, you're *Standing At the Edge of the Water*—the water of Powerful Anointing. Please don't allow yourself to be complacent or satisfied with your spiritual growth, but come across the river. An anointing is awaiting that will make you a mighty force for the sake of the Kingdom of God.

You can be a champion, one who will put spiritual forces to flight through the anointing of the Holy Spirit.

CHAPTER 8

THE WATER
OF RESTORATION

There is perhaps no other passage in all the Bible that is as well known or as well loved throughout the world as is the psalm of David that is frequently known as the "Shepherd Psalm."

Among scholars, there is some disagreement about exactly when Psalm 23 was composed, but I'm persuaded that it was probably written toward the end of David's life as he looks back over the course of his days. This isn't the song of a young boy full of wide-eyed optimism. Rather, one of a seasoned veteran who has experienced life to the fullest and has discovered in all of its changes that the Lord is the Shepherd who is truly all-sufficient.

One of the first things we see in this psalm is that it is written from the viewpoint of a sheep. It's as though the animal was musing over its life spent among the flock, being protected by a shepherd, and recording its feelings and observations. The key thought upon which the entire psalm rests is the very first statement: *"The Lord is my shepherd, I shall not want."*

Here, David refers to God as *"The Lord."* This is the translation of *Jehovah,* which was the most respected and loftiest title that a Jew could utter. That name was considered so holy and sacred that whenever the Jewish people publicly

106

read the Scriptures and came to that name they would substitute some lesser title for God rather than even pronounce or speak that word aloud. It's been said that when they would copy the manuscripts, the priest would first wipe off his pen and say a prayer of blessing over his life before he would even dare to write the hallowed name down on parchment.

Jehovah means the *I Am*—the self-existent Being. He who inhabits eternity and has life in Himself. The title *Jehovah* consists of three tenses of the Hebrew verb "to be." And in combining those three, He is revealed as He who *was*, He who *is*, and He who *will be.*

The name signifies God as the Eternal One—the One who is continually becoming to His children all that they need until, at last, the Word becomes flesh. This is the God of all gods, the supreme Creator of all that is, the self-existent, self-sustaining Divine Being before whom everything else bows and from whom all else receives its existence.

And *Jehovah* isn't just the name for the Supreme Being of the universe, it is a covenantal recognition. *Jehovah* is the One with whom there is a covenant of blessing and protection. It is also a name of relationship—a bond that He makes with those who are His own.

When the Lord says to Moses, *"I AM that I AM"* and He presents Himself as *Jehovah,* He is letting him know, "I'm going to reveal Myself to you in a way that nobody has ever known Me before. It's a relationship. It is a covenant I make with you." Thus it is that He proclaims Himself in His Word as *Jehovah.*

Then God adds another title with it that describes the *qualities* and the *kind* of relationship we have with Him and He has with us.   He is *Jehovah-jireh*—the Lord who sees to it; who provides for all the needs of His people. No longer should we worry or fear. There is no need to be anxious,

107

constantly wondering what the future holds, because He's going to see to all our needs. In addition:

- He reveals Himself as *Jehovah-tsidkenu*—the Lord our Righteousness. He imparts this to us so that we become the righteousness of God in Christ.
- He reveals Himself as *Jehovah-m'kaddesh*—the Lord our Sanctifier. When we are unable to enter into His presence because we are defiled, He divinely touches us so that we are made holy, even as He is holy.
- He reveals Himself as *Jehovah-shalom*—the Lord our Peace. This isn't just the absence of conflict, but it's wholeness and completeness in all our being.
- He reveals Himself as *Jehovah-rophe*—the Lord our Healer. He is the One who heals the bitterness of our lives and causes it to be sweet once again.
- He reveals Himself as *Jehovah-sabaoth*—the Lord of Hosts. He is the mighty, warring Lord who fights our battles and conquers the enemy that tries to prevail against us.

This is the Lord who is in relationship with us; our Shepherd. This is the God who makes a covenant of blessing and protection with His people who are called the sheep of His pasture. This Almighty, self-existent Jehovah is MY Shepherd. And because He is, I shall not want for anything. There is never any reason to be afraid, uncertain, or insecure.

This is an important truth to grasp, because there are men and women who view the Lord as A Shepherd, but they really don't know that the Lord is THEIR Shepherd.

If you have not understood Him to be YOUR shepherd then you're never quite sure if He's going to come through for you. There remains that nagging doubt in the back of your mind that constantly questions, "What about now? What about the situation I'm in and the problem I am facing today? What about tomorrow?"

But when you have an absolute confidence and assurance the Lord is your Shepherd, then you can boldly, without any reservation, declare, "I shall not want." Because He is my Shepherd:

- My Shepherd supplies.
- My Shepherd cares for me.
- My Shepherd protects me.
- My Shepherd watches over me.

Gone is the apprehension and fear. You can *relax*—which may be the best word you've heard all week!

THREE STEPS TO RESTORATION

As we look at the first section of Psalm 23 please observe the beautiful picture of how the Great Shepherd is caring for His children: *"He makes me lie down in green pastures; He leads me beside quiet waters. He restores my soul..."* (verses 2-3).

First: HE MAKES US REST

Sheep, by nature, are rather timid creatures. They are frequently alarmed and will actually run over each other racing away from something that startles them. The way the shepherd corrects the problem is by catching a sheep and gently, yet firmly, forcing it to lie down and feed quietly on the grass beneath its feet.

I've discovered that sometimes it is necessary for the Lord to impose an enforced rest on you and me. We live in a

109

hectic, hurried age; a time when headache medications have become best-selling national products. In the midst of this chaotic world, there are days we sometimes must be *made* to lie down by our Shepherd.

Perhaps you feel like you've been placed in God's enforced "time-out." You may have been a mover and a shaker, always in the thick of things—used to making everything happen, part of the "in" crowd, the inner circle of people in the know. But now you feel like you've been placed on the shelf. The phone doesn't ring like it once did. Life isn't as exciting as it used to be. You feel "stuck" in a rut. Everything seems so ordinary. The crowd is gone; the information bypasses your desk; you're out of the loop. And the worst part of it is, you are lonely.

- Just because you're lonely doesn't mean you are alone.
- Just because you're on the shelf doesn't mean you are not useful.
- Just because you're in "time-out" doesn't mean your time is over.

God does some of His best work when we are by ourselves—when we're still and isolated. This period of rest is nothing more than the Lord *making* us lie down in His green pastures because He has something exciting planned just around the corner.

You may think that where you are is dark, that life has passed you by and you have no future, but the Lord has put you in a place of rest for a purpose. He has lessons He wants you to learn. This is not the end; it is preparation for the next season into which God is getting ready to usher you.

The fields in which He makes us lie down are *green*, nourishing, strengthening pastures. Our heavenly Father doesn't force us to lie down where we can't survive; He is fortifying and building up our soul and spirit.

Just coming to the house of God—even when it seems like a chore and we don't want to make the effort to go there—just sitting and soaking in the presence of God is a part of His green pasture rest. In the company of believers He nourishes us.

Second: HE LEADS US BESIDE QUIET (STILL) WATERS

We are at the edge of the water again. Perhaps you thought when the Lord led you here it would be white-water rafting time, or you imagined the waves would be crashing and you'd be surfing. Maybe you thought the river would be rushing and you'd be caught up in the current of His Spirit.

You've been hoping for excitement and grand, glorious times. But all you have is this quiet stream, a small pool of still waters. And you're wondering what you're doing here. Of all places—why *here*?

It is the Lord who has brought you to this place of rest and has led you beside quiet waters. It is for a specific reason that you will experience what comes next.

Third: HE RESTORES OUR SOUL

You have come to the Water of Restoration. Think about that for a moment. In fact, I invite you to pause, take a deep breath, close your eyes, quietly exhale, and repeat these words: *"He restores my soul!"*

When we talk about the soul we are referring to our mind, our thoughts, our personality, and our will. We are also speaking of our emotions, our ability to think, decide, reason and feel.

The marvelous assurance of Psalm 23 is that He restores our mind, will, and emotions. And He doesn't accomplish this in the middle of a crowded mass, rather, He gets us alone, makes us rest, and leads us beside still waters.

The word *restore* is a far stronger term than it seems on the surface. It literally means: *He brings back my soul.*

THE SHEPHERD'S SHEEP

A sheep does not have the strength of a lion, nor is it swift-footed like an antelope, or smart like a dog. The notable characteristic of a sheep is that it's not very intelligent; that is why we call them "dumb sheep."

When a sheep goes astray it does so for no reason, and once it starts wandering off, it can rarely find its way back home.

Throughout the Bible we are told the Lord is the Shepherd and we are the sheep.

- That's the meaning of Psalm 100:3: *"We are His people and the sheep of His pasture."*
- That's the meaning of Psalm 78:52: *"But He led forth His own people like sheep, and guided them in the wilderness like a flock."*
- That's the meaning of Jeremiah 50:6: *"My people have become lost sheep; their shepherds have led them astray. They have made them turn aside on the mountains; they have gone along from mountain to hill and have forgotten their resting place."*
- That's the meaning of Ezekiel 34:11-12: *"For thus says the Lord God, 'Behold, I Myself will search for My sheep and seek them out. As a shepherd cares for his herd in the day when he is among his scattered sheep, so I will care for My sheep and will deliver them from all the places to which they were scattered on a cloudy and gloomy day.'"*

- That's the meaning of Jesus' words in John 10:27-28: *"My sheep hear My voice, and I know them, and they follow Me; and I give eternal life to them, and they will never perish; and no one will snatch them out of My hand."*

Since God calls us His sheep, it gives special significance when we hear the prophet Isaiah say: *"All of us like sheep have gone astray, each of us has turned to his own way; but the Lord has caused the iniquity of us all to fall on Him"* (Isaiah 53:6).

The Lord has brought us to the edge of the water because we've gone astray in our thinking. He has us here in order to bring us back to our right mind; so the former thoughts no longer dominate our thinking.

We've bought into the message that is being presented by the culture of our day that says, "It's all right; we just weren't compatible. So I'm going to find someone else."

But the Lord counsels: "Your thinking is wrong. I've called you to the water's edge because I want to bring you back to your right mind."

The Bible tells us, *"There is a way that seems right to a man, but the end thereof is the way of death"* (Proverbs 14:12).

Sadly, we've accepted the thinking of society that believes, "If it feels good do it. It'll be okay." No. It's *not* okay!

We've been conditioned to accept this idea: "I have these cravings and desires that need to be satisfied." That may be true, but along the way there has been some "stinking thinking" that crept in. It's time for people to have what I call "saved brains."

We have believed the negative words that have been said

to and about us. It's no wonder we are upset, depressed, and our self-esteem is shot!

The Lord has called us to the edge of the water because He wants to bring us back to right thinking. When He does, we will begin to realize who we are, how God sees us, and what He says about us.

RESTORING OUR MIND

Millions have fallen into the trap that, "It's all about me. And if I weren't involved, nothing would get done."

We've stood condemned because we believed the lies our spiritual enemy has been whispering in our ear. He constantly reminds us of how we once were; the sinful stuff we used to do; and all the times we've fallen. When we attempt to do something for God, Satan will jump up and ask, "How in the world can you stand and lift your hands, singing songs of praise, when you are guilty of all that garbage in your past?"

But remember, God has us at the edge of the water and He is trying to get through to us—to bring back our *MIND* and restore our soul.

We haven't seen anything take place like we thought it would and we begin to doubt that the Shepherd even cares. Our trust has eroded and our thoughts are overrun with fear and foreboding, worrying that nothing will ever be any different than it is right now.

But the Lord has led us to the *quiet* water and has made us lie down. There's nothing exciting happening and it seems very vanilla. That is because He wants to have our full attention and bring us back to a right mental attitude. He desires to restore our thinking and remind us that He hasn't forgotten about us.

Where we find ourselves today is not our final destination,

but one that is needed because there are some issues that we need to get right with God. He's waiting to renew and refresh our mind so that the negative is washed away and replaced with a positive confidence—not in what we can do, but in what He will do through us.

The Lord longs for us to be still and know that He is God. He wants us to cease striving in our own strength and remember the Lord God Almighty who is awesome and majestic—to understand that His supernatural acts in the past were wonderful and that the purpose was accomplished in its time. But the new thing He's getting ready to do is so much greater that we can't possibly compare it to yesterday.

In Isaiah 43, the prophet proclaimed a word of hope for the people of Israel: *"I have redeemed you. I've called you by name; you are mine. When you pass through the waters, I will be with you; and through the rivers, they will not overflow you. When you walk through the fire, you will not be scorched"* (verses 1-2).

Following this amazing promise, the message of the prophet continues as he talks about the marvelous things God did for His children—leading them safely through the Red Sea, delivering them from captivity, bringing down the chariot, the horse, the army, and the mighty men.

Then in verse 18, God gives a startling exhortation: *"Do not call to mind the former things, or ponder things of the past."*

Wait a minute! That's *our* heritage. Those wonderful things happened to *us*. One of the ways we knew it was God is because of the great miracles that were performed.

Then the Lord says, "Behold!" This means we are to sit up and pay attention. *"Behold I will do something new, now it will spring forth; will you not be aware of it? I will even make a roadway in the wilderness, rivers in the desert"* (verse 19).

God is telling us that what we experienced in Him was

indeed grand, and we should praise Him for it. But as marvelous as it used to be, we must leave it in the past, because the Lord has a brand new path on which He's getting ready to lead us.

What handicaps and keeps us stuck at the starting line is the fact that we keep expecting the Lord to re-do and re-create everything that He's already accomplished. We fail to understand that we ought to celebrate and rejoice over what God has done, then we should tuck these things away, leaving them in a box of remembrance.

Why? Because God says, "When I get ready to do My next thing, it will be new and different. There will be some of the same elements. It's going to be My Spirit. Everything will line up in agreement with My Word, but it will arrive in a different package; to you, it may seem unusual in the way it looks, acts, walks, and sings."

The Lord declares, "I've got something new. And as long as you keep looking for what I have done in days gone by, you will miss what I am doing now."

God desires to lift us into realms of His presence and His Spirit that we've never known before. But if we keep hanging onto yesterday and say, "If He doesn't do it that way, it's not God"—we will miss His blessing.

It is difficult to learn new things in the midst of ceaseless noise clamoring for our attention. They can only be revealed in the quiet, secret place...beside still waters.

When there are no distractions, we can meditate on God's Word—which is truth—which will put to flight all the inconsistencies of the world's arguments and will truly set us free from every negative onslaught.

I've never understood why those who claim to be Christ-followers are more willing to believe a secular psychologist than what the Word of God declares, or why Christians will embrace what the media promotes and talk-show hosts suggest over God's holy Word.

The Word of life isn't revealed in the news reports or the internet headlines. It's not found by following the tweets of the rich and famous, or even revealed in the so-called positive circumstances that seem to accompany our wrong choices. It's only found in God's Word.

In the quiet place we can ponder and pray over the Word that will set us free from every adverse influence—where we discover over and over again just how much He really cares for us.

RESTORING OUR WILL

Not only is the Lord restoring our mind, but He has us in the place of rest because He is also restoring our *WILL*.

Like sheep we have gone astray. We've made wrong choices and often have used our will to make decisions that are in opposition to God's perfect plan.

One of the reasons we fail to see more of the dynamic working of the Almighty is because we have tried to tell God how to operate. We have set the parameters and marked the boundaries, building a box and expecting the Lord to stay within it. We praise God for how He works—as long as He does it according to our will.

What we do not understand is that the Lord won't stay within our limitations, nor is He interested in doing so.

The only time we are ever going to really see the release of the powerful work of God is when we break down the walls of our box in which we have grown comfortable, throw up our hands in surrender and cry out—"*Not my will, but Your will be done.*"

A major problem Jesus had with the Pharisees of His day was that they wouldn't accept the will of God. They couldn't see how God could come to earth as a Man. The Lord of

117

Glory descended in physical form and wanted to tabernacle with them, but they rejected His will and His way. They had built a very rigid, religious container out of rules, laws, ordinances, regulations, and commandments. They couldn't imagine the Lord would work outside of those narrow confines.

The truth is, we haven't made a great deal of progress since those early days. We see the working of God through our own lens, we define it by our own criteria, and measure it by our own grid. Anything that falls outside the parameters of personal experience, we discount and even actively resist.

The Lord is trying to teach us that He isn't bound and limited by the walls we erect. Sometimes the very thing that is most outside our comfort zone is what He will use to bring about the greatest breakthrough and the most significant demonstration of His power, glory, and grace in our lives.

The Lord—the covenant-making, covenant-keeping God —has us at the edge of the water because He wants to restore our will. At the very place where we keep choosing a crooked path, even when we know it is wrong and can't seem to help ourselves, He has brought us here to make us whole so our will is once more in alignment with His.

RESTORING OUR EMOTIONS

Finally, I want you to know the Lord has us standing at the edge of the water because He is restoring our *EMOTIONS.*

God is working on both extremes. He's bringing back to wholeness those who are overly emotional, and He is bringing back to wholeness those who are cold and emotionless. This includes men and women who feel everything to the extreme: who have been hurt, wounded, and scarred; who are a jumble of nerves; who are grieving and can't seem to find comfort; who are depressed; who are frightened and anxious.

- Hear the voice of the Great Shepherd as He proclaims through the words of the prophet: *"Surely our griefs He Himself bore, and our sorrows He carried; yet we ourselves esteemed Him stricken, smitten of God, and afflicted. But He was pierced through for our transgressions, He was crushed for our iniquities; the chastening for our well-being fell upon Him, and by His scourging we are healed"* (Isaiah 53:4-5).
- Hear the voice of the Great Shepherd as He gently whispers: *"Come to Me, all who are weary and heavy-laden, and I will give you rest. Take My yoke upon you and learn from Me, for I am gentle and humble in heart, and you will find rest for your souls. For My yoke is easy and My burden is light"* (Matthew 11:28-30).
- Hear the voice of the Great Shepherd as He instructs through the words of the Apostle: *"Humble yourselves under the mighty hand of God, that He may exalt you at the proper time, casting all your anxiety upon Him, because He cares for you"* (1 Peter 5:6-7).
- Hear the voice of the Great Shepherd as He announces through the song of the Psalmist: *"Bless the Lord, O my soul, and all that is within me, bless His holy name. Bless the Lord, O my soul, and forget none of His benefits; who pardons all your iniquities; who heals all your diseases; who redeems your life from the pit; who crowns you with lovingkindness and compassion; who satisfies your*

years with good things, so that your youth is renewed like the eagle" (Psalm 103:1-5).
- Hear the voice of the Great Shepherd as He sings through the Psalmist: *"You have turned for me my mourning into dancing; you have loosed my sackcloth and girded me with gladness, that my soul may sing praise to You and not be silent. O Lord my God, I will give thanks to You forever"* (Psalm 30:11- 12).

To the person who is afraid to let down your guard and feel anything because it seems something has died within you; to the individual who has hardened your heart and decided the best path to take is the one of stoicism, determined to never be in a place where you can be hurt again—hear the voice of the Great Shepherd as He encourages you to dare to dream once more.

The valley you are in right now is by perfect design. Know that the God who placed you here has determined to bless you. He has decreed good things and made a covenant of blessing and protection with you. The Lord is committed to your well-being .

God is trying to renew and refresh your spirit, to restore your soul. He's bringing back your mind, your will, and your emotions. He is returning them to the original design specifications of the Manufacturer.

You may be in the valley where there is not much activity. The waters are quiet and still—but God's at work. He is molding, fashioning, and shaping you into His image. He's restoring your soul.

CHAPTER 9

THE WATER OF WHOLENESS

Harry was a quiet, unassuming man with a quick smile and bushy, handlebar moustache. What began as a single sore on the top of his balding head quickly spread until his entire face and most of his head was covered with raw, oozing skin cancers.

Before a Sunday service in our church his wife pulled me aside and asked if I would please say special prayers for him that week. At the conclusion of the meeting, as the couple was exiting, I felt prompted that this was a good time to trust God for His healing, so I asked several of the church members to join me and lay hands on Harry, believing God for a miracle of healing grace.

On Thursday of that week I received a phone call from Harry. "Pastor, I just wanted you to know that my skin has cleared up until there is only one little spot left—and it's almost healed as well."

The next Sunday Harry was back in church, smiling broader than ever. Standing before the congregation he testified, "God has touched and healed me. For the first time in months I've been able to shave without cutting myself. My skin is smooth like a newborn baby. God is so good!"

A MIRACLE IN THE MAKING

We don't even know her name. She was a slave; a Jewish captive in the household of Naaman, commander of the Syrian army. This young girl seems like the most unlikely candidate to be the catalyst for a miracle, but her actions tell us she was a person of compassion and deep faith.

Even though highly successful and wielding considerable power, Naaman had contracted the dreaded disease of leprosy. It was through the testimony of this unnamed maid from Israel that he learned of a God greater than leprosy; a God who is a healer that takes great delight in making sick people whole.

The name, Naaman, means *pleasant/agreeable*. And here we discover a life lesson that tells us that it doesn't matter how good, well-liked, well-mannered, or successful we may be, sickness and disease is no respecter of persons. Some of the nicest people fall ill—while some of the meanest seem to stay healthy. I don't know if meanness drives away sickness or if there is any correlation between the two, but some of the most pleasant, most agreeable people do indeed become sick.

In this story (2 Kings 5:1-14) we are told that Naaman and his entourage began a journey to Samaria to find this prophet who might heal him. Naaman took with him ten talents of silver and six thousand shekels of gold, plus ten changes of clothes as a gift. One person has calculated that the value of those gifts was approximately $75,000. That's a lot of money by today's standards, but it reminds me that you can't put a price on health and healing.

When you are sick—especially when it's a disease as disfiguring or terminal as leprosy—no amount of money is too much to pay. We may complain about the cost, but we gladly shell it out if it will mean we can regain our health.

I think it's significant that a slave maid was the one to tell her master about the miracles that could happen through the prophet, because the truth I've discovered is that God's word of life will often come through unexpected and unlikely sources.

When the Syrian army came and raided this girl's village, she didn't for one minute think that her misfortune might become the means for the healing of her captor. All the time she was likely frightened, wondering what was going to happen to her, and I'm sure her parents were worried over her well-being—but God had a miracle in the making.

Had she not been taken captive, Naaman wouldn't have received his healing; we would not have this story, and we would miss a powerful truth that can change our lives.

To those who are in need of a physical touch this narrative powerfully reminds us that the Lord offers healing grace. He takes great delight in bringing health and wholeness to our physical bodies.

HEALING FOR BODY AND SOUL

However, this story isn't just about a physical illness. In the Bible, leprosy is more than a dreaded disease; it represents something far worse. Leprosy is incurable by any human means. It is a "wasting" disease that is contagious, eating away until the flesh is destroyed. As such, it is a type and representation of sin.

We find leprosy listed in the Hebrew Law. It is the one disease which required the involvement of a priest to determine that the person is indeed leprous, then the priest prescribed rituals of sacrificial offerings for cleansing if the leprosy disappeared (see Leviticus 14).

One of the most significant points we learn when we read the entire account of Naaman is that not only is he cured of the physical disease of leprosy, but there is also a spiritual

123

transformation that occurs in his life. Jumping ahead in the narrative, after he is cured, Naaman returns to Elisha and tells him, *"Behold now, I know that there is no God in all the earth, but in Israel"* (2 Kings 5:15).

Before his cleansing, Naaman was a pagan idolater. Not only does the Lord heal his body, but he leaves the Jordan with a fresh revelation of God and discovers not just a change of body, but a change of heart. He tells the prophet, *"...your servant will no longer offer burnt offering nor will he sacrifice to other gods, but to the Lord"* (verse 17).

The story of Naaman is a spiritual type and shadow of salvation. Sin is a wasting disease, and it is fatal. We can't cure ourselves of sin, nor can we purchase our salvation. There is no way we can be good enough to remove the stain of sin from our life. The only remedy is a work of the Lord's mercy because iniquity can only be washed away by a miracle of God's grace.

Naaman couldn't be healed by washing in the clear waters of the streams of Lebanon. It had to be the muddy Jordan. It couldn't be waters that were from the land of the pagans, even though they may have been pleasant and inoffensive. In this case, cleansing could only come from what was flowing in God's holy land.

So it is that our salvation (our cleansing and wholeness) can't derive from the pleasant places of this world. It doesn't matter how appealing the counsel is, or how agreeable the alternatives seem, we can only be made free and complete when we come to an old rugged cross. As we kneel at the foot of that cross we will discover:

> *There is a fountain filled with blood*
> *drawn from Immanuel's veins,*
> *And sinners plunged beneath that flood*
> *lose all their guilty stains.*
> (William Cowper, 1771)

Perhaps you carry emotional scars from bitter words that have been said to you, about you, or actions done to you. It could be that the wounds are the result of unwise and wrong choices you have made, or from a direct attack of the spiritual enemy who seeks to destroy all that God has intended for good.

You've discovered that no matter how hard you try, you can't heal yourself of emotional hurts. There is still the free-floating anxiety, the innate fear, the crushing intimidation. You come to the conclusion that your thinking is still being shaped by negative events from your past and your reactions are still being colored by abuses suffered at the hands of others.

Perhaps it's a family issue or a relationship struggle. There are many situations where we can't solve our problems. Let me boldly proclaim to you that even though you cannot bind your own wounds, there is healing and wholeness available through the miracle in-breaking of the grace of Almighty God, by the power of His eternal Spirit.

FORGET YOUR PRECONCEPTIONS

The story of Naaman speaks of both physical and spiritual wholeness. When God takes control, no matter where we are broken, we will be made whole.

One of the lessons we learn from this account is that we can miss the hand of God because it doesn't conform to our preconceived ideas of how the Lord will work.

Naaman almost missed out. The Bible records, *"So Naaman came with his horses and his chariots and stood at the doorway of the house of Elisha. Elisha sent a messenger to him, saying, 'Go and wash in the Jordan seven times, and your flesh will be restored to you and you will be clean.' But Naaman was furious and went away and said, 'Behold I thought, "He will surely come out to me, and stand and call on the name of the Lord his God, and wave his hand over the place, and cure the leper"* (2 Kings 5:9-11).

Naaman had a preconceived notion of how this whole thing was going to shake down. He had worked it all out in his mind. He had imagined how it would look: "I'm going to drive up in my chariot...and the man of God is going to come out of the house...he's going to stand in front of me and pray an eloquent prayer to his God. Then he is going to wave his hand over the part of my body where the leprosy has broken out...and I'm going to be cured."

But that's not what took place. Elisha didn't even bother to walk to the front door. He didn't anoint him with oil, lay hands on him, or even pray. The prophet didn't do any of the things a good Pentecostal would say you have to do in order to see people healed—not one thing! He just sent a ridiculous message through his servant: "Go and wash in the Jordan."

The Jordan! Of all places, why the Jordan? Why not some place clean, cool, and sparkling like Abanah or Pharpar? Why not one of the rivers of Damascus? The idea of the Jordan was so disgusting, Naaman, *"...turned and went away in a rage"* (verse 12).

I've often wondered how many times people have missed the wholeness God wanted to bring to their lives because they were unwilling for the Lord to do it His way instead of theirs. Men and women miss salvation because they're attempting to come to God by their good works, their membership in a club, their standing in the community, or by their heritage. But they refuse to accept God's way—the way of the cross.

- How often have people missed their healing because the prayer line looked too long and disorganized?

- How many times have people missed their break-through because God's plan of praise wasn't in their vocabulary?
- How many times have people missed their wholeness because they were waiting on somebody else to ask them for forgiveness instead of following God's plan and taking the first step?

In truth, the healing wasn't found in the water—but in the act of obedience.

And so, here we find Naaman—*Standing At the Edge of the Water.* Part of him is upset, complaining, "This is the dumbest thing I've ever heard." Another part of him is thinking, "What have I got to lose, except this disease?"

Thankfully, that's the part that prevails—and he steps into the water.

"SEVEN DUCKS IN MUDDY WATER"

I never read the story of Naaman without thinking about my mother. Mom didn't consider herself a preacher, however there were a few occasions when she was called upon to fill the pulpit for my father. The one sermon I have the notes on from my mother is a message on Naaman that she titled "Seven Ducks In Muddy Water."

In her message she labels each of the times Naaman dips in the water. Each of these becomes a step that forms a process for wholeness to be completed.

Naaman dipped himself in the Jordan the first time—and it was a dip of FAITH.
Hebrews 11:6 tells us, *"Without faith it is impossible to please Him, for he who comes to God must believe that He is and that He is a rewarder of those who seek Him."*

The faith that pleases God is that which not only believes that He exists, but also that He will respond and reward those who diligently seek Him. It is not just the assurance that God makes people whole—it's believing that God will make YOU whole.

Naaman dipped the second time—and it was a dip of HUMILITY.

Here was a captain of the Syrian army, a mighty warrior who was in control and command. We see him dipping himself in the muddiest of rivers with an entire battalion of men looking on. What a humbling experience.

When we get desperate and reach the end of our resources, we won't really care what anybody else thinks. Pride flies out the window. This is why James 4:10 reminds us, *"Humble yourselves in the presence of the Lord, and He will exalt you."*

Naaman dipped a third time—and it was a dip of OBEDIENCE.

Sometimes the only motivation we have for being involved in spiritual things is obedience. We don't feel the tug of faith and it may seem a bit foolish. It certainly looks ridiculous, when we've been believing, confessing, and proclaiming, but there's been no answer.

It is in those times that obedience keeps us walking in the right direction. God's Word tells us, *"If you are willing and obedient, you shall eat the good of the land"* (Isaiah 1:19 NKJV). And we know that Christ *"became to all those who obey Him the source of eternal salvation"* (Hebrews 5:9).

Naaman dipped a fourth time—and it was a dip of SUBMISSION.

It is at the point of submission that we admit, "I give up.

It is not my way—it's Your way. It is not my will—it's Your will. It is not my strength—it's Your strength." Remember, *"'Not by might nor by power, but by My Spirit,' says the Lord of hosts"* (Zechariah 4:6).

Naaman dipped a fifth time—and it was a dip of DELIVERANCE.

Once we move through faith, humility, obedience, and submission, we are brought to the place of *deliverance*. I have found that many stop here, but if we do, we will never be made whole. Oh, we may have freedom, but we will not have the power and the joy we want and need. We will wonder why it is we are still empty and continually plagued with the same temptations over and over again.

God doesn't just want to bring us out, He desires to bring us in. The Lord doesn't just long to bind up and cast out that which is causing the problem, but He wants to loose His presence and His power to fill the empty place.

Don't stop with deliverance, because there's still more of God required to make you whole. If we slam on the brakes here, somewhere down the road our spiritual enemy is going to return and find the house swept and cleaned, but nobody's occupying it. And Satan will bring seven more spirits worse than the one we had to deal with before.

Press on—go down into the waters again. There is still more of God you need in order to be whole.

Naaman dipped a sixth time—and it was a dip of PERSEVERANCE.

When things get better, when the enemy gets off your back, when the load lightens and the pain diminishes, some feel they have received everything they need. But this is not what the Lord intends. He is asking you to persevere and follow His command until you have completed *all* the

Word of the Lord.

If God tells you to shout—a mumbled "Praise the Lord" won't do. If He asks you to repent—He needs more than a meek apology.

Half obedience is *NO* obedience! If you fail to receive the promise the first time you pray—keep praying. Keep confessing, believing, and holding onto the promise. Never allow the enemy to steal the destiny that has already been placed in your spirit by God.

- If you're in the valley, *persevere* until He restores your soul.
- If you're in the dead of night, *persevere* until joy comes in the morning.
- If you're in the depths of discouragement, *persevere* until He turns your mourning into dancing, gives a garland instead of ashes, and a garment of praise for your spirit of heaviness.

Refuse to give up. Refuse to give in. Persevere!

Naaman dipped a seventh time—and it was a dip of PERFECTION.

If God says dip seven times, don't stop with five or six.

The final time Naaman went down in the water, the Bible says that his flesh was restored like the flesh of a little child. He was made perfect—body, soul, and spirit.

This is God's assurance to you today: *"For I am confident of this very thing, that He who began a good work in you will perfect it until the day of Christ Jesus"* (Philippians 1:6).

His promise is to make you whole!

CHAPTER 10

THE WATER OF VICTORY

"We don't need or want any more churches in this community!" With those words from an irate resident echoing in my ears, I slowly drove away from the county planning board meeting.

Ours was a new church plant, just a few months old. I was a young, inexperienced pastor. The mother church had given us five acres of land on which to construct a worship facility, but the zoning had to be changed. And now here were citizens lining up to oppose what we were certain was the will of God. They had caught the ear of the commissioner representing that region who had pledged to never vote in favor of another church being built in that community. It was going to be an uphill battle—with no guarantee of success.

The final meeting with the county commission was in two weeks. With limited resources, and even less ability, I did the only thing I knew to do—I called the church to prayer. We were convinced that God had led us to that place for that time. We also believed that the battle wasn't just over traffic flow and property values, but it was a spiritual fight with consequences for souls in eternity.

The night of the meeting arrived and the room was

packed. I made the appeal on behalf of the church to the best of my ability, but when I sat down I just knew I hadn't been nearly persuasive enough to have our petition granted. Sitting in that chamber, I prayed under my breath, "Lord, this is Your church. I've done all I can do. I need Your help."

Those who wished to speak to the issue were given the opportunity. The first person to the microphone was the very individual who had been so vehement in opposition at the previous meeting. I sat in amazement as I listened to this person who had been so articulate before, now rant and rave almost incoherently; unable to put two sentences together in a manner that made any sense.

Each person who rose to speak in opposition to the measure sounded confused and distracted while everyone who spoke in favor came across as reasoned and polished.

It finally came time for the vote—and the commissioner who had vowed to never favor another church was the person who made the motion for approval. The vote was unanimous! Today there is a wonderful congregation that continues to worship and minister on that property.

As we reflected on the process, we were made to realize that the outcome wasn't due to our political maneuvering, but it was because of divine intervention. The battle wasn't ours—it was the Lord's. Through Him, the victory was won.

ANYTHING BUT MATH!

When I was in school, my weakest subject was math. I hated math! I think it is from the pit! Give me Geography, Biology, History, or English; anything but math.

I can recall on more than one occasion being in a Geometry or Algebra class where I slaved and sweated blood trying to get the proofs of an equation or attempting to factor out a number—and getting it wrong. Often it would look like I had performed all the necessary calculations correctly, but the result wouldn't be what was on the answer sheet. The teacher would look it over and, at first glance, it would seem okay, but when the equation was carefully examined, there would always be some point where I had left out a step or where I had forgotten to completely factor a part of the equation.

That's what I think about when I read this very familiar story from Bible times. In this situation, there is a problem which presents itself, but one of the people involved makes the mistake of not completely factoring the equation. As a result, the individual comes up with an incorrect answer that proves disastrous.

In 1 Samuel 16, David has been anointed as king over Israel in a secret ceremony by the prophet, Samuel. Then, at the end of the chapter, God orchestrates the circumstances so that David is brought into the royal palace.

When chapter 17 opens, the Philistines, who are the sworn enemies of Israel, are once again tormenting the people of God. They have come out in full battle array against Israel.

This conflict wasn't fought like we might think battles should be. Instead of each soldier engaging the first enemy he saw, the opponents would draw up the lines that separated each side. Often there would be a contest between the two fiercest warriors—and it was a "winner-take-all" match. The side whose champion won would be the masters and the side whose champion lost would be the servants.

So here we have Israel and the Philistines in a face-off. The Philistines lauded their hero, a giant whose name was Goliath, from Gath. He was the stuff of which your worst nightmare is made—taller by a couple of feet than an NBA center, and muscles double the size of the reigning Mr. Universe. He was huge! This giant was an army all by himself—"a lean, mean, fighting machine."

For 40 days Goliath had been taunting the army of Israel and challenging them to send out their champion for hand-to-hand combat. Every day, morning and evening, Goliath issued his challenge. He would curse and blaspheme the Lord God and taunt and humiliate the Israelites. During these days Israel huddled in foxholes while Goliath flexed his muscles, boasted of his prowess, and roared his defiance of all they considered sacred and holy.

Saul is king—and everyone in Israel was looking to him to save them. After all, Saul was the tallest warrior among them; the Bible describes him as being head and shoulders above the rest (see 1 Samuel 9:2).

However, there is a problem. The Spirit of the Lord had departed from Saul, and as a result, he's just as terrified as everybody else!

WHICH SIDE OF THE BROOK?

Into this scene David arrives. And he, who is filled with the Spirit of God, an anointed servant of the Lord, can't understand why all the men of the army are so fearful. So David volunteers to fight this giant, and when they determine that his offer is serious, word is sent to King Saul.

As we read the account, we learn that first Saul tries to give David his personal armor, but it was too big for the lad. David wasn't accustomed to wearing such bulky battle gear, so he shunned the protection in favor of his shepherd's sling and set out across the valley to face the giant.

On his way, David stopped at the edge of a brook—and it's a defining moment for him. If he stays on *this* side of the brook, he's in a comfort zone. There is no risk. He can hide in a foxhole along with everybody else, or return to tending his father's sheep, even occasionally visiting the palace and playing his harp for the king. Nobody expects much from someone so young and inexperienced anyway, so it would be no disgrace to turn back.

But once he crosses the brook, he is committed. Something—no, *everything*—has to change once he crosses to the other side. David is *Standing At the Edge of the Water.*

He bends down and selects five smooth stones and places them in his shepherd's pouch. Now David didn't pick up five stones because he was uncertain of his aim. Neither was he unsure that God was really going to come through and bring about the victory. What's the difference anyway if you're fighting a giant with stones flung from a shepherd's sling? One stone...five stones...none of them are going to be very effective without some kind of supernatural help.

There are a couple of reasons I can think of why David picked up five stones. First of all we find out later that Goliath isn't an only child; he has siblings and other relatives. So David didn't really know if he was going to have to fight only Goliath or his entire family. It is always best to be prepared.

But there's a second reason why "five stones" has significance. In the Bible numbers have meaning, and five is the number of GRACE.

Grace is the undeserved favor of God. Grace is also His operational power—the means by which the Lord does His mighty work.

When David picks up five stones, it's an admission that he can't possibly hope to win this battle in his own strength. He will need supernatural empowerment; the power of God working on his behalf. These five stones are a statement that the battle isn't his, but the Lord's. It is a declaration that it's "not by might, nor by power, but by the Spirit of the Lord" (see Zechariah 4:6) that the victory will be won:

- It's a statement that, "Greater is He who is in me than he who is in the world" (see 1 John 4:4).
- It's a statement that, "No weapon that is formed against me will prosper" (see Isaiah 54:17).
- It's a statement that, "With God, nothing is impossible" (see Luke 1:37).
- It's a statement that, "God's grace is sufficient for me" (See 2 Corinthians 12:9).

So David has his grace assurance; the stones are safely in the bag, he crosses the brook, and runs to meet Goliath.

When the giant sees him approaching, his mental wheels start churning. He's checking out the situation; measuring his opponent. And when Goliath surveys the boy coming to meet him, he starts doing the calculation and concludes that the scales are obviously tipped in his favor. His chances of victory are so great that it seems almost absurd to go through with the contest. He almost defeats himself by laughing too hard and can't believe this is the best Israel can muster. He was looking forward to matching up against King Saul, not some mere boy from the flocks.

You make the comparison:

- Goliath is a giant—David a mere lad.
- Goliath is an experienced warrior—David is a shepherd and a musician.
- Goliath is wearing hundreds of pounds of armor—David a leather tunic.
- Goliath comes to battle with a spear, sword, and a shield—David is armed with a sling and a staff.

This is going to be a massacre!

After assessing the situation and factoring the problem, the giant assumes what to him is the obvious answer; he will win without breaking a sweat. It's so ridiculous that he belly-laughs—and his laughter is heard all through the valley. In fact, it strikes terror in the hearts of those in the camp of Israel. You can almost hear King Saul back in his tent as he laments, "What have I done sending a mere boy to fight?" He covers his eyes and says, "Tell me when it's all over and we have to surrender."

David, on the other hand, sees the scales tipped as well. But when *he* looks at the situation, he sees things leaning in *his* favor. We are told why when he reveals the part of the equation that Goliath forgot: *"You come to me with a sword, a spear, and a javelin, but I come to you in the name of the Lord of hosts, the God of the armies of Israel, whom you have taunted"* (1 Samuel 17:45).

Saul, cowering in his tent, saw a giant too big to fight. David saw a giant too big to miss.

THE THREE PARTS OF THE EQUATION

We already know the outcome, so let's factor all of the elements to see how the victory was won:

The first part of the equation is the IMMEASURABLE POWER OF GOD.

David said to the giant, "I know things don't look good for me and you think I'm weak and inexperienced. But I also know there is a detail you have ignored. The Lord God of my fathers has promised that when I go in His name, under His banner, He will fight for me. So I am not here in my own

137

strength, but I come in the name of the Great Jehovah. And God and I are a match for anybody!"

This is a message we need to hear today, because too many believers spend their entire lives in the same condition as the army of Israel—cowering in a foxhole, terrified at the bravado of the enemy. We are engaged in a spiritual battle with an adversary who attacks our lives. He seeks to destroy us: physically, emotionally, psychologically, and most important, spiritually. He attempts to tear apart our homes and families—and tries to rob us financially, doing his best to see that we are vanquished. The Bible describes him as a *"thief"* who comes to *"steal, kill and destroy"* (John 10:10).

Many who claim to be Christ-followers live in a state of confusion, frustration, and depression because they are overwhelmed by the tactics and the power of this spiritual enemy. They are terrified by the odds that are stacked against them and by circumstances over which they feel they have no control.

TOO BIG FOR THE LORD?

As a child growing up in church I can vividly remember having what we called the "devotional service" and "testimony meetings." I still recall people standing to "testify"— and the whole time they were talking, they did nothing but relate how abusive the devil had been to them that week.

Even today, some of the men and women I am asked to counsel visit my office and all they dwell on is their problem and how they can't take the pressure any longer.

There are times when I have requests to pray with an individual for deliverance. Somehow they seem to think if the right person would just lay their hands on them...and if they could just get the devil off their back...then their troubles would all be solved.

When I hear this kind of complaining, I want to jump up and shout, "Where is God in all of this?" We major in minors and minor in majors, leaving out a vital part of the equation.

It may surprise you to know that none of us are designed to be strong in our own abilities. Our Creator never intended for us to be able to single-handedly cope with the problems of life. Instead, He encourages us to become weaker and weaker until we eventually die to self. It is only when we empty ourselves of any power we think we have that He can replace it with His divine strength.

That is what the Apostle Paul is teaching us when he writes, *"...power is perfected in weakness"* (2 Corinthians 12:9). It's what he means by saying, *"...when I am weak, then I am strong"* (verse 10). It is also the focus of Hebrews 11:34, which speaks of the heroes of the faith who *"from weakness were made strong."* We are further instructed to be *"strong in the Lord and in the strength of His might"* (Ephesians 6:10).

God wants us to look at *every* aspect of the equation. When we do, we will recognize who the Lord is; His mighty strength and ability. We also begin to see that Satan is a defeated foe and has no real authority, because Jesus declared, *"All authority has been given to Me in heaven and on earth"* (Matthew 28:18).

This is confirmed in Paul's letter to the believers at Ephesus: God raised Christ *"from the dead, and seated Him at His right hand in the heavenly places, far above all rule and authority and power and dominion, and every name that is named, not only in this age, but also in the one to come. And He put all things in subjection under His feet, and gave Him as head over all things to the church, which is His body, the fullness of Him who fills all in all"* (Ephesians 1:20-23).

As I was writing this I tried to think of a problem that is so insurmountable or unsolvable that God can't handle.

Some time ago there was a report of how scientists were concerned about a huge sheet of ice in Antarctica that was showing signs of melting. They were trying to calculate how much the seas would rise over the earth if this vast amount of ice were to melt—estimating it might be anywhere from 11 to 20 feet. And for a moment I wondered if that much water added to the sea would present a problem God couldn't handle. Then I read Isaiah 40:12 where the prophet tells us that the Lord has *"measured the waters in the hollow of His hand."*

I watched with curiosity and interest the progress of the space shuttle mission where the astronauts were performing complicated space walks while working on repairs to the Hubble Telescope so they could get better pictures of the universe. And I pondered whether figuring the size and make-up of the universe would present an insurmountable problem for God—until I saw in the same verse that He *"measured off the heavens with His fingers"* (NLT).

I read and hear the reports about the growing concern over the effects that global warming will have on the environment, crops, and gravitational pull. Some even believe the mountains may start to crumble. I wondered if such a disaster would pose a problem too big for the Creator—until I continued to read that God *"calculated the dust of the earth by the measure, and weighed the mountains in a balance, and the hills in a pair of scales."*

This is the all-powerful God:

- Who *"hangs the earth on nothing"* (Job 26:7).
- Who *"counts the number of the stars [and] gives names to all of them"* (Psalm 147:4).

- Who rides *"upon the the wings of the wind"* (Psalm 18:10).
- Who *"sits upon the flood"* (Psalm 29:10 KJV).

THE GOD FACTOR

Recorded in the Old Testament is the account of an elderly couple with the names of Abraham and Sarah. They had a promise from God that they would have a child together (Genesis 17:16), but Abraham was almost 100 years old and his wife was nearly 90. To the natural mind, this seemed impossible. But when God speaks, miracles happen—and Isaac was born.

In the days when Jesus walked the earth, there was a woman who for 12 years had been suffering with what the Bible refers to as an "issue of blood" (Mark 5:25-34). She had been to every doctor, specialist, and treatment center available. Nobody could help her. But when she received word that Jesus was in town, she pushed her way through the crowd, and with her last ounce of strength she touched the hem of His garment. Immediately, the hemorrhaging stopped, and she discovered the Son of Righteousness had risen with healing in His wings.

Then there is the heart-rending story of a little girl who was seriously ill. Her father, Jairus, pleaded with Jesus to journey with Him to her bedside (Luke 8:40-42; 49-56). But before they reached the house, word reached them that his daughter had died. When they arrived, the mourners were already there and the mortician had been called. The young girl was laid out on the bed and the sounds of weeping echoed through the house.

But Jesus assured them, "Don't worry. Everything is going to be fine."

141

Immediately, those present began to ridicule Him, thinking He had lost His mind. Then Jesus cleared the room, stepped over to the bed, took the girl by the hand, and commanded her to rise. Instantly, she sat up and was reunited with her parents. When the dead girl sits up, the funeral's canceled!

I am at a loss to think of a problem God can't handle.

- No resources? The meal barrel will not be depleted and the oil bottle will not run dry.
- No money? The fish has a coin in its mouth.
- Fed to the lions? The angel shuts the animals' mouths.
- Thrown into the fire? The Fourth Man walks in the midst of the furnace and gives protection.

When you find yourself on the front line of a battle, never forget to factor in the *power* of God.

The second part of the equation is our SECURE POSITION IN HIM.

- According to John 1:12: *"...as many as received Him, to them He gave the right to become children of God, even to those who believe in His name."*
- According to Colossians 2:12: We have been *"buried with Him in baptism [and] raised up in Him through faith..."*
- According to Romans 8:15: *"...you have received a spirit of adoption as sons by which we cry out, 'Abba! Father!'"*
- According to Romans 8:17 (NKJV): We are *"heirs of God and joint heirs with Christ..."*

- According to 1 Peter 2:9: *"...You are a chosen race, a royal priesthood, a holy nation, a people for God's own possession, so that you may proclaim the excellencies of Him who has called you out of darkness into His marvelous light."*

How blessed we are that we can stand on the truth of Scripture, knowing that we are saved, sealed by the Holy Spirit unto the day of redemption, and are part of God's forever family. Because of His mercy, He has saved us by His grace and has raised us up with Jesus and seated us with Him in the heavens! (see Ephesians 2:4-6).

That is our *POSITION.* We're one of the King's kids. God doesn't want us trembling in a foxhole, flinching at shadows, fearful, confused, frustrated, or depressed. Instead, He desires to seat us with Christ Jesus in heavenly places.

God designed us to win, created us to overcome, and destined us for victory. That's why He wants us to start seeing things from His perspective, so we understand that our spiritual adversary has already been defeated.

The power of the Almighty is greater than the enemy —and our position in Him is secure.

The third part of the equation is the UNFAILING PROMISE OF HIS WORD.

Perhaps there are giants looming in your life at this very moment. Circumstances are difficult and adversities are too numerous to count.

You may be *Standing At the Edge of the Water.* On this side you've learned to cope with the way things are. It may not be picture-perfect—and might be somewhat humiliating.

Hold on! The Lord wants you to know that this is *not* the way it was meant to be. It's *not* what He had in mind when

He called and brought you out of darkness into light. So pick up the stones out of the brook. Cross over the water; face your fears, and in His might, confront your giants.

Never engage the battle in your own strength, but move forward in the name of the Lord. And when you do, He promises that He will fight *for* you. The giant has come against you, but it isn't really you he's fighting. You are a child of the King—and the war is against God Himself. So step out in His name and He will fight on your behalf.

- This is God's promise: *"Be strong and courageous! Do not tremble or be dismayed, for the Lord your God is with you wherever you go"* (Joshua 1:9).
- This is God's promise: *"When the enemy comes in like a flood, the Spirit of the Lord will lift up a standard against him"* (Isaiah 59:19 NKJV).
- This is God's promise: *"And my God will supply all your needs according to His riches in glory in Christ Jesus"* (Philippians 4:19).
- This is God's promise: *"He brought me up out of the pit of destruction, out of the miry clay, and He set my feet upon a rock making my footsteps firm. He put a new song in my mouth, a song of praise to our God"* (Psalm 40:2-3).
- This is God's promise: *"Weeping may last for the night, but a shout of joy comes in the morning"* (Psalm 30:5).
- This is God's promise: *"[You can cast] all your anxiety on Him, because He cares for you"* (1 Peter 5:7).
- This is God's promise: In every situation, through every test, and in every circumstance, you're not going down in defeat, but you are going to *"overwhelmingly conquer through Him who loved [you]"* (Romans 8:37).

THE DIVINE SOLUTION

Here's the equation: the immeasurable *POWER* of God, plus our secure *POSITION* in Christ, plus confidently acting on the *PROMISES* of God's Word which cannot fail, equals *VICTORY* every time.

I don't know which part Goliath omitted, but he surely missed a vital element. When we read the end of 1 Samuel 17, we see the final outcome. The giant hadn't just challenged Israel's army, but he had blasphemed the name of Jehovah. This wasn't merely a territorial dispute over land to decide who was going to be in power—it was a holy war. It was a battle to determine not which nation was greater, but which *GOD* was greater.

When David factored the Lord God into the equation, Goliath fell and the army of the Philistines was routed.

Whatever foe you may be facing today, never forget to include God in the computation. He makes all the difference.

The contrast between those who live with confidence and courage and those who never seem to rise above the level of their problems has nothing to do with a superior intellect, a better "hot-line" to God, a more prestigious social pedigree, or an abundance of material possessions. The determining factor is that those who are making it—those who are victorious—are the men and women who have stepped across the water's edge. They have picked up the stones for their sling, faced their fears, and confronted the giant.

But they haven't relied on their personal skill with the sling, the accuracy of their vision, or the strength of their arm. Instead, they have trusted completely in the Lord and allowed themselves to be tools and instruments in His hands.

They may have feelings of weakness, foolishness, and even timidity, but because they have included God in the equation, they are able to stand tall.

You can be a giant-killer if you work the equation.

The POWER of God
+ Your POSITION in Christ
+ Acting on the PROMISES of the unfailing Word of God
_____
= Always equals VICTORY.

You may be *Standing At the Edge of the Water*, uncertain if you want to take on the daunting challenge of fighting Goliath. Let me encourage you. When you operate in the name of the Lord, it is not even a risk—you are assured of triumph. The giants in your life *will* fall and you *will* be victorious.

So: Face Your Fears. Fight Your Giant. Finish the Task.

CHAPTER 11

THE WATER
OF PRAISE

Pain is an experience with which we are all too familiar. None of us is exempt. It comes in many different forms, shapes, and sizes—debilitating illness, broken relationships, shattered dreams, a bankrupt business, a destroyed career, betrayal of a friend, the death of a loved one.

There are many reasons why we hurt. Some are in anguish because of things that have been done to them over which they had no control.

Pain is not always caused by others; it can result from the tragedies and adversities of life. No doubt you've experienced this: you're going along just fine when something happens that knocks all the wind out of your sails. It can be an accident that wasn't your fault, or that of anyone else. It was just *LIFE.*

Some hurt because there is a spiritual enemy whose objective is to kill, steal, and destroy. The moment we decide to live for Christ and follow Him as a true disciple, we become a prime target for Satan's arrows. When he shoots them our way, he can wound, tear, and create terrible pain.

Often, the greatest anguish we experience is that which we bring on ourselves; the consequence of our personal behavior. Such is the case described by the writer of Psalm 137.

If ever there was a song written in the minor key, it's this one from the ancient hymn book. The writer is a POW who has been exiled to Babylon. With tears blurring his vision and a catch in his throat, he begins to remember the helpless, hopeless feeling of despair and the bitter humiliation suffered at the hands of his captors.

He writes: *"By the rivers of Babylon, there we sat down and wept, when we remembered Zion. Upon the willows in the midst of it we hung our harps. For there our captors demanded of us songs, and our tormentors mirth, saying, 'Sing us one of the songs of Zion'"* (verses 1-3)

The rivers of Babylon were mighty currents indeed. On the east was the Tigris—a river first mentioned in connection with the Garden of Eden. Upon its bank was built Nineveh, the capital of Assyria.

Then there was the Euphrates—also connected with the Garden of Eden. It flowed through the center of Babylon. Past and future conquerors of Israel all held the rivers of Babylon in the heyday of their power. In fact, the vast kingdoms of Persia, Greece, and Rome became world empires in the prophetic sense of the Bible only when they held the Euphrates River.

Here were the Jewish exiles. They had been marched northward and eastward; mile after endless, weary mile. The last scene etched in their minds had been the smoke rising from the ruins of their beloved city, and especially of their most cherished possession—the Temple. Now they had arrived in "the land between the rivers." It was by the waters of Babylon, they sat down and wept.

The pain was exacerbated by the knowledge that their captivity was caused by their own disobedience to God. Following the death of King Solomon, the united kingdom of the Jewish nation had split into the 10 northern tribes (known as Israel) and the 2 southern tribes (known as Judah). Every one of Israel's kings led her away from God. Even though Judah experienced times of revival, the fact is that only 8 of her 20 kings were righteous men. In spite of repeated warnings, the people of God were determined to follow their own path. The result was that first Israel fell to the Assyrians and later Judah was captured by the Babylonians.

In his insightful book, *Living the Psalms*, Chuck Swindoll describes the dreadful scene: "I can just hear the taunts of the Babylonian guard as he looked out over those downcast, depressed people of Judah. 'Hey, how about all you Jews joining in on one of those good ol' hymns of the faith! Let's hear it for dear ol' Jehovah! Sing it out now...and as you sing, remember Zion!'"

FACING THE CONSEQUENCES

It seems we live in a time in which precious few want to take personal responsibility for their own actions. When things go wrong or when pain is inflicted, it's always the fault of something or someone else. We've become very good at assigning blame as long as it is away from ourselves. If we're caught in a wrongful act we may be remorseful, but too often what we're *really* sorry about is not the sin we committed, but that we got *caught* doing it.

Somehow, we forget that our actions always bring consequences. And when our behavior is *wrong*—especially in the eyes of God—the penalty can often be severe. The wisdom writer tells us, *"...the way of the transgressors is hard"* (Proverbs 13:15 KJV). And the Apostle Paul gives this warning: *"Do not be deceived, God is not mocked; for whatever a man sows, that he will also reap"* (Galatians 6:7).

Even though sin may be forgiven, the aftermath often lingers, causing difficulties. We can accept Christ and find forgiveness, yet still need to take care of the baggage we carry

149

as a result of our days as a transgressor. There may be a financial mess to untangle, a broken relationship to mend, a crushed spirit to revive, or a debt to society to repay. All of those things, and more, are part of taking personal responsibility for our own actions.

When we repent of our sins, immediately, our past is forgiven. According to God's Word, not only are the sins pardoned, but the Lord forgets them and they are removed as far as the east is from the west. However, the men and women around us don't necessarily forget. And when the crisis involves a broken trust, it always takes time for that bond to be rebuilt. It doesn't automatically happen just because we received forgiveness from the Lord; there is a process. The consequences of sin are terrible; the way of the transgressors is indeed hard.

Israel found herself by the waters of Babylon because she had sinned and refused to follow God. The nation turned a deaf ear to the prophets when they thundered onto the scene and proclaimed, "Repent! Turn away from idols and turn back to God!"

The Israelites did the same thing some do every Sunday in church. The Word of the Lord is proclaimed and God speaks to us concerning dealing with the issues in our lives. But we say what Israel said: "Not today."

Make no mistake; there is coming a point of reckoning—a time when we will discover that we reap what we sow. In fact, the law of sowing and reaping says that we will always reap *more* than we sow. That's what the Old Testament prophet meant when he said, *"They sow the wind, and they reap the whirlwind"* (Hosea 8:7).

Israel's exile by the waters of Babylon wasn't designed solely for the purpose of punishment or retribution. Rather, the time spent there was God's discipline—part of His mercy and grace. Even in the midst of captivity, the Lord wasn't finished with Israel.

- They might be in Babylon—but they were still the people of God.
- They might be in bondage—but they were still His children.
- They might be discouraged and distressed—but they were still His chosen ones.

You see, justice means you get what you deserve. If Israel had received justice, they would have been totally wiped out. But mercy says you *don't* get what you deserve. And grace goes even further and means you get the *goodness* that you don't merit.

Even in the hardship of Babylon, Israel was receiving mercy and grace. They were being introduced to a dimension of God they had never before understood. They were learning:

- Something about His heart of compassion.
- Something about His protection in the midst of persecution.
- Something about the depth of His lovingkindness they would never have known outside the land of captivity.

Babylon was God's discipline. He was using whatever it took to get Israel back into a right relationship with Him so His blessings could once more be showered upon her. God was saying, "I know that you are in Babylon right now and it's because I have had to correct you as a result of your disobedience. But I want you to learn the lesson that this captivity is only temporary. The same God who allowed you

151

to go *in* is the same God that's going to see to it that you are brought *out.* I will see to it that blessings will once more flow to your land."

HOW CAN WE SING?

The truth is that when we find ourselves in the long, dark night of the soul—whether it's from wounds that have been inflicted upon us by others, or anguish that is the result of the consequences of wrong choices, it is a painful place to be. Whatever route brings us to the land of captivity, bitter disappointments, hard trials, and distress, most of us can identify with the psalm writer when he asks, *"How can we sing the Lord's song in a foreign land?"* (Psalm 137:4). How can we sing the Lord's song:

- —in the time of grief?
- —in the time of despair?
- —in the time of desperation?
- —in the time of adversity?
- —in the time of weakness?
- —in the time of hurt?
- —in the time of loneliness?
- —in the time of broken dreams?
- —in the time of our spirit being crushed?
- —in the time of trial?

As I reflected on how the Israelites could sing the Lord's song while struggling under Babylonian captivity, I was struck by the thought: *Where else are we supposed to sing the Lord's song if not in a foreign land?*

Even if everything's going your way and there are blue skies and fair winds—even if you're in the place of plenty and the land of blessing, anything this side of eternity is still foreign territory. But this is not the end of the line. This is not our ultimate destination, or our final resting place. We're still pilgrims and strangers, seeking a city whose builder and maker is God.

- The Lord's song is a song of victory.
- The Lord's song is a song of triumph.
- The Lord's song is a song of confidence in the One who has called us unto Himself.
- The Lord's song is a song of witness, testimony, and praise that will turn the hearts of even the heathen to worship of Almighty God.
- The Lord's song is one that says, "I haven't arrived yet...but I'm on my way to Canaan's land."
- The Lord's song is one that proclaims, "I haven't yet obtained the promise...but I'm still marching to Zion."

That's what Paul and Silas understood so well in Acts 16. Here they were—falsely accused, unjustly beaten, chained, and thrown into the Philippian jail. Their feet were securely fastened in the stocks and the prison doors were bolted and barred. But at midnight, they lifted up their parched voices and began to sing the Lord's song in a foreign land. Their chorus of praise caused shackles to break, stocks to loosen, prison doors to open, and a pagan jailer and his household to be saved.

REJOICE! REJOICE!

The reason we can sing, even in a foreign land, is very simple. We are not singing the Lord's song because of where we are, but because of where we're going. We have caught a glimpse of the future—and it is beyond amazing.

For this reason, when Paul was coming to the end of his life in a Roman prison, instead of lamenting his fate and crying about his negative circumstances, he shouts: *"Rejoice in the Lord always; again I will say, rejoice!"* (Philippians 4:4). This is why the apostle could write: *"...in everything give thanks; for this is God's will for you in Christ Jesus"* (1 Thessalonians 5:18).

I am not singing because I'm here—I'm singing because of where I am headed. At the moment, I may be in a place of discipline. Perhaps I made some wrong decisions and am reaping the consequences because of the Lord's correction, but I can sing His song since I remember that, according to Hebrews 12:6, the Lord only disciplines those He loves. And because He loves me I know that the time of chastisement isn't the final end, but it's a means of bringing me into conformity with His will and His way.

I'm on my way to being conformed to His image and likeness; to bearing *"the peaceful fruit of righteousness"* (Hebrews 12:11).

Even during a time of trial I can lift my voice with the song of the Lord. According to James 1:2-4, *"Consider it all joy, my brethren, when you encounter various trials, knowing that the testing of your faith produces endurance. And let endurance have its perfect result, so that you may be perfect and complete, lacking in nothing."*

To be honest, I'm not really thrilled about the time of testing, but the end result of enduring the trial is that I will one day be complete in Him. Even if I go through the fire I'm not going to be destroyed, but instead I will come forth as pure gold.

I may be in the foreign land of affliction, yet His song rises within me because I recall 2 Corinthians 4:16-18: *"Therefore we do not lose heart, but though our outer man is decaying, yet our inner man is being renewed day by day. For momentary, light affliction is producing for us an eternal weight of glory far beyond all comparison, while we look not at the things which are seen, but at the things which are not seen; for the things which are seen are temporal, but the things which are not seen are eternal."*

When we find ourselves in the midst of affliction we have a tendency to feel that nobody has ever had it as bad as we're experiencing at the moment. We phone our best friend, whining and moaning about our situation. Then we call the pastor, the elders, and anyone else we think of who will listen to our tale of woe.

But as bad as it is, the above verse calls it a *"momentary, light affliction."* In other words, it's temporary, not eternal.

My outer man is decaying, but I wish there was an x-ray or an MRI that would let you see my inner man. On the outside I'm just a 175 lb. weakling, but on the inside I've got bulging biceps. I'm benching 350 lbs, running 5 miles and not even getting winded. The reason I am a powerful specimen on the inside is because I've been willing to say, "Okay, Lord. I don't like the problem, but even now, I will sing your song because what I'm going through is producing an eternal weight of glory far beyond all comprehension."

My troubles aren't easy to bear, and I certainly wouldn't wish them on anybody else, but as difficult as my circumstances are, they are nothing compared with the rejoicing that awaits me.

A BRIGHTER PATH

I understand what it's like to be in the long dark night of the soul. I understand what it's like to have people turn against you and to stand in sorrow at the graveside of a loved one. But I also know the peace that comes with making a conscious decision that says, "I don't like what I'm going through right now, but God is still God. He is still my heavenly Father, and I'm still His child."

Regardless of the trials, it doesn't change the dynamic or alter the truth that I am His and He is mine. The fact is: I'm not going to be here forever.

- I refuse to get stuck in my grief.
- I refuse to get stuck in my depression.
- I refuse to get stuck in my anxiety.

Praise God, I'm headed somewhere else. The Lord has a light at the end of the valley. He has a better day, a brighter path, a different dimension, a new season for my life, and I'm walking into it. So while I am in my present situation, I'm going to sing His praises—not because of today, but because of tomorrow.

I may be in the foreign land of desperation and destruction, but even here I can raise my hands and sing because I remember the words of the Psalmist: *"I waited patiently for the Lord; and He inclined to me and heard my cry. He brought me up out of the pit of destruction, out of the miry clay, and He set my feet upon a rock making my footsteps firm. He put a new song in my mouth, a song of praise to our God; many will see and fear and will trust in the Lord"* (Psalm 40:1-3).

I may be in the foreign land of fear, but even there I can sing the Lord's song. Psalm 46 reminds us: *"God is our refuge and strength, a very present help in trouble. Therefore we will not fear, though the earth should change and though the mountains slip into the heart of the sea; though its waters roar and foam, though the mountains quake at its swelling pride. There is a river whose streams make glad the city of God, the holy dwelling places of the Most High. God is in the midst of her, she will not be moved; God will help her when morning dawns. The nations made an uproar, the kingdoms tottered; He raised His voice, the earth melted. The Lord of hosts is with us; the God of Jacob is our stronghold"* (verses 1-7).

In the midst of fear, stress, and worry, I'm singing the Lord's song because I am headed to my eternal home; a place of security and strength—where the God of Jacob is my refuge and my Rock.

LIKE A DREAM

I constantly deal with men and women who are struggling. They are at a loss as to how to get out of their "pit." While I am certainly not trying to be dismissive of your heartache, I want to help you understand that the pain you're in at the moment is not the final destination. There's a better way, and a better day coming.

When we become wrapped up in the negative, our song seems to vanish. When we are hurting, the last thing we want to do is sing—but that is exactly what we *should* do.

For those bound in captivity, let me turn your attention to Psalm 126: *"When the Lord brought back the captive ones of Zion, we were like those who dream"* (verse 1).

If you've ever been in a place where you were hurting and struggling and then you were set free, it doesn't even seem real. It's as if one morning the anguish was all there; even when you went to bed that night it was still present—but when you woke up the next morning the burden was lifted. It seemed like a dream.

As the children of Israel, we *were* sitting by the rivers of Babylon, weeping. We had hung our harps on the willow tree and refused to sing the song of the Lord. But when God brought us back from captivity to Zion, it truly *was* like a dream, but that wasn't the end of the story. Now they could

157

rejoice, saying: *"Then our mouth was filled with laughter and our tongue with joyful shouting; then they said among the nations, 'The Lord has done great things for them.'* (And we responded,) *The Lord has done great things for us; we are glad"* (Psalm 126:2-3).

Can't you see them dancing in the streets of Jerusalem? Before this, they were sitting by the waters of Babylon, crying, "Woe is us! Woe is us!" But then the Lord brought them back and it seemed like they were in a fog. Yet they were filled with laughter, shouting for joy, and dancing in the streets. All because of the awesome miracles the Lord had done for them.

The psalmist continues, *"Restore our captivity, O Lord, as the streams in the South"* (verse 4). They knew what it was like to sit by the rivers of Babylon and weep in their captivity, but now they were praying for the Lord to bring them to another stream—one of complete freedom. This is why he could write, *"Those who sow in tears shall reap with joyful shouting. He who goes to and fro weeping, carrying his bag of seed, shall indeed come again with a shout of joy, bringing his sheaves with him"* (verses 5-6).

When the Lord frees you and brings you out of bondage, it won't be only you that leaves that horrible life behind—you are going to be able to reach out to some folks around you and say, "Come with me. We're going back to the Father's house, to the land of blessing."

It's not just about us, rather all that *concerns* us. So we have some "sheaves" to bring along.

Perhaps you feel like those enslaved Israelites and you have lost your song. It's as if your joy has flown out the window and you're wondering how you're going to just make it through the rest of the day, let alone try to sing the Lord's song. God is saying to you: "It's time you pulled your harp off the limb of the willow tree and tuned the strings. Lift your voice and sing My song of praise once more. Not because of where you are, but because of where you are going!"

The moment the Lord hears that melody of praise, He will break the shackles of your bondage. Your mouth will be filled with laughter and your tongue will shout for joy. Once more, the Lord will cause streams to flow in your desert!

STEP INTO THE WATER

On these pages you have been challenged to lift your eyes and see:

- The Water of Deliverance
- The Water of Blessing
- The Water of Promise
- The Water of Provision
- The Water of Decision
- The Water of Life
- The Water of Powerful Anointing
- The Water of Restoration
- The Water of Wholeness
- The Water of Victory
- The Water of Praise

It is my prayer that as a result of reading this book and asking for the Lord's guidance and direction, you will no longer be simply *Standing at the Edge of the Water*—you will step out in faith and experience the victory that is waiting for you on the other shore.

FOR ADDITIONAL RESOURCES OR TO
SCHEDULE THE AUTHOR FOR SPEAKING
ENGAGEMENTS, CONTACT:

JOHN V. MORGAN
1677 SOUTHSIDE BLVD.
JACKSONVILLE, FL 32216

PHONE: 904-725-1234
EMAIL: pastorjohn@regencychurch.org